Come and Learn of Me

To understand and maturing in the things of God you must know that it is a process!

"In order to go up you must grow up"

By

James L. Monteria

CLM Publications & Publishing, LLC
P.O. Box 932
Chesterfield, Va 23832

Come and Learn of Me

All rights reserved. No part of this book may be reproduced without written permission from the publisher except for use of brief review for furthering of the Kingdom of God unless otherwise indicated; all Scriptures are taken from the King James Version of the Bible

CLM Publications & Publishing, LLC
P.O. Box 932
Chesterfield, VA 23832
www.clmpublication.info
ISBN: 978-0-9821450-6-7

Cover Design/Graphics: Shelly E. Middleton
Author: James L. Monteria
Associate Editor: Jennifer Valentine and others
Published by CLM Publications & Publishing, LLC

Copyright © 2010 by CLM Publications & Publishing, LLC Printed in the United States of America; All rights reserved under International Copyright Law. Contents and cover may not be reproduced in whole or in part in any form without the expressed written consent of the publisher.

Table Contents

Chapter 1 Man in the Vision	Page 1
Chapter 2 What is this Peace that I am Experiencing?	Page 5
Chapter 3 What Is this Love that I am Feeling?	Page 11
Chapter 4 How Does God's System Operates?	Page 21
Chapter 5 Who is God's enemy and how does He operate?	Page 38
Chapter 6 Two Kingdom on one Plant	Page 45
Chapter 7 The Makeup of Humankind "Spirit\Soul\Body"	Page 60
Chapter 8 Faithfulness, Consistency, Diligence and Excellence	Page 75
Chapter 9 Introduction to Spiritual Maturity	Page 84
Chapter 10 Step 1 Faith	Page 95
Chapter 11 Step 2 Virtue	Page 112
Chapter 12 Step 3 Knowledge of God	Page 124
Chapter 13 Step 4 Temperance "(Self-control)"	Page 139
Chapter 14 Step 5 Patience	Page 147
Chapter 15 Step 6 Godliness	Page 157
Chapter 16 Step 7 Brotherly kindness	Page 176
Chapter 17 Step 8 Charity (Agape) God kind of Love	Page 192
Decision Pages	Page 205
Bibliography	Page 208
Partnership	Page 215
About the Author	Page 218

Acknowledgement

Primarily, my understanding of God and my ability to articulate any thoughts about Him are solely attributable to His grace and mercy. It is through the profound experience of God's grace, the Lordship of Jesus Christ, and the active presence of the Holy Spirit in both my life and ministry that I have come to a deep and abiding appreciation. The significance of these divine elements surpasses mere verbal expression, as their influence is deeply embedded in both my personal spiritual journey and my ministerial endeavors.

Foreword

In sharing the message of Jesus as articulated in Matthew 11:28-30, Jesus invites us with the words: "Come unto me, all ye that labor and are heavy laden, and I will give you rest. Take my yoke upon you and learn of me; for I am meek and lowly in heart: and ye shall find rest unto your souls. For my yoke is easy, and my burden is light." This passage underscores the invitation to find spiritual rest and solace through a relationship with Jesus, characterized by His humility and gentleness.

Many Christians possess a limited understanding of salvation, often perceiving it primarily in terms of eternal life—an anticipation of what awaits them beyond this earthly existence. However, a thorough examination of Scripture reveals that eternal life begins at the moment of salvation, encompassing numerous benefits that are intended to be experienced in the present, as part of our daily life.

Salvation extends beyond the promise of eternal life to include a range of spiritual blessings and practical benefits that are available to believers here and now. Understanding and embracing these benefits allows Christians to fully integrate the transformative power of salvation into their everyday lives, aligning their daily experiences with the divine promises of rest, peace, and renewal offered through Jesus Christ.

Jesus said...
Come and Learn of Me

To understand and maturing in the things of God you must know that it is a process!

"In order to go up you must grow up"

Chapter One
Man in the Vision

In 1984, I experienced a significant encounter while attending a service at Grace Fellowship Church, where Pastor Bob Yandian was delivering a sermon. Although I do not recall the exact title of his message on that particular Sunday morning, the atmosphere was imbued with a profound teaching anointing, which is a customary feature of the services at Grace Fellowship. During this service, as I was immersed in the presence of the Lord and attentively absorbing the teachings of the Word of God, the Spirit of God imparted to me a vision. This vision, which I have since come to understand, addressed a profound theological question: "What transpires within an individual when they accept Jesus, the Christ, as their personal Lord and Savior?"

As I sat there, the Holy Spirit revealed to me a vision of a man who appeared to be heavily burdened by the cares of life. His facial expression was contorted, and his countenance vividly reflected a state of utter desperation and the associated anguish. In this revelation, the man's posture suggested that he was bearing an immense load upon his back, symbolizing the weight of his burdens.

It seemed as though the Spirit of God granted me the ability to perceive the contents of the metaphorical bag he was carrying, thereby illustrating the nature and magnitude of the man's afflictions.

Within this large, heavy bag were the burdens, cares, troubles, and problems that had accumulated throughout his life, creating a profound sense of despair. Each step he took seemed fraught with difficulty, as if it might be his last. As I observed, the man appeared to be ascending a gentle hill toward the cross upon which Jesus had been crucified. Upon reaching the summit, he knelt down to pray.

It was at this moment that a noticeable transformation occurred; his countenance, once marked by pain and distortion, became radiant and serene, reflecting a newfound sense of peace and relief.

A tangible sense of peace enveloped him, and as he began to walk away from the cross, it appeared as though his thoughts were materializing visibly above his head. This phenomenon resembled the thought clouds commonly depicted in cartoon comic strips, where a cloud-like figure symbolizes the character's inner contemplations.

The first thought was:

A cloud-like figure materialized above his head, as if revealing his innermost thoughts. The first thought that emerged was, "What is this freedom and peace that I am experiencing?" He marveled at the complete absence of his previous burdens, cares, troubles, and problems. Overwhelmed with joy at this newfound sense of freedom, yet another cloud-like figure appeared, again revealing his thoughts: "What is this love that I am feeling?" It seemed as though he was filled with an overwhelming desire to embrace everyone he encountered. Additionally, he felt a compelling urge to share this newfound love with others. As he continued walking, more profound questions arose within him, signaled by another cloud-like figure: "How does God's system operate?" and "Have I failed by trying to live according to the world's system?"

Finally, he pondered, "Who is God's enemy, and how does he operate?"

As I observed this individual moving forward after receiving Jesus as his personal Lord and Savior, I could see that he was reflecting on these various thoughts, with different questions continuously coming to his mind.

It was as though the Lord was engaging in a dialogue with him, saying, "Now that you have encountered Me, I invite you to 'Come and Learn of Me.'" Inspired by this vision, I wish to elucidate what Jesus intended when He extended the invitation to the man in the vision: "Come and Learn of Me."

Matthew 11:28-30.

> Come unto me, all *ye* that labour and are heavy laden, and I will give you rest. [29] Take my yoke upon you and learn of me; for I am meek and lowly in heart: and ye shall find rest unto your souls. [30] For my yoke *is* easy, and my burden is light.

"Where *there is* no vision, the people perish: but he that keepeth the law, happy *is* he."

Proverbs 29:18

Chapter Two

What Is This Freedom/ PEACE That I Am Experiencing?

I would like to engage in a scholarly reflection on the man from the vision and the profound question he posed to himself: "What is this freedom and peace that I am experiencing?" Through a critical examination of the Scriptures, we can ascertain the transformative events that unfolded in the life of this individual. Furthermore, this exegetical inquiry allows us to comprehend the theological and existential dimensions of the peace he encountered, demonstrating that this profound sense of peace is not only attainable but universally available to all who seek it.

Jesus entered the world with a clearly defined and distinct mission: He was born with the ultimate purpose of dying. His death on the cross was not merely an arbitrary event, but rather divinely preordained and theologically essential, as a significant price was required to redeem humanity from the bondage of sin.

The contemplation of death, however, often provokes discomfort, a response rooted in the fundamental nature of human existence. According to biblical anthropology, humanity was originally created for eternal life, not death.

This is reflected in the discomfort associated with mortality, for death was not part of the original divine design. As articulated in Romans 5:12, death entered the world through Adam's disobedience. In response to this rupture in the created order, God sent Jesus to die on the cross as a means of restoring humanity to life, thus reestablishing the potential for eternal communion with God.

Romans 5:12, *"Wherefore, as by one man sin entered into the world, and death by sin; and so death passed upon all men, for that all have sinned:"*

During His earthly ministry, Jesus meticulously adhered to the law and courageously proclaimed the Gospel. Despite His obedience and moral perfection, He was still required to suffer and ultimately die. Jesus' death stands as perhaps the most profound instance of injustice in human history, as He was entirely undeserving of such a fate. His death was not the consequence of His own wrongdoing, but rather, as the prophet Isaiah prophesied, "the Lord laid on Him the iniquity of us all" (Isaiah 53:6). This profound act of substitutionary atonement underscores the theological conviction that Jesus bore the sins of humanity, taking upon Himself the punishment meant for others, thereby fulfilling the divine plan of redemption.

Jesus endured the profound suffering of the cross in order to secure cleansing and deliverance for humanity from the bondage of sin. The man in the vision, though unaware at the time, experienced reconciliation with God by accepting Jesus as his Lord and Savior. This act of reconciliation signifies the restoration of a relationship between humanity and the divine, a relationship fractured by sin. All of humanity, as the Scriptures affirm, stands guilty before God, and it is solely through the redemptive work of Jesus Christ that we are granted peace with God, thus enabling us to experience the peace of God. This peace, along with many other spiritual blessings, is promised to believers, as reflected in the prophetic and apostolic writings: "the chastisement for our peace was upon Him" (Isaiah 53:5), "My peace I give to you" (John 14:27), and "the fruit of the Spirit is love, joy, peace" (Galatians 5:22) *"But the fruit of the Spirit is love, joy, peace, longsuffering, gentleness, goodness, faith"*

The Bible affirms in Psalm 29:11, "The Lord will bless His people with peace." In the vision, the force that Lucifer—also referred to as Satan or the devil—used to manipulate the man was the spirit of fear. Scripture explicitly identifies fear as a spiritual entity, stating, "God hath not given us

The spirit of fear" (2 Timothy 1:7). Although living in perpetual peace may seem an unattainable ideal to the world, the Bible suggests that such a state is indeed possible for those who are in communion with God.

The human heart possesses an inherent longing for peace. This is evidenced by the persistent global efforts of organizations and governments to establish peace among warring factions and nations. Across cultures, people desire to live in harmony rather than in conflict. However, despite humanity's tireless endeavors to secure peace, the world continues to be marked by unrest and discord. This position underscores the limitations of human efforts to achieve true peace, a peace that the Bible asserts can only be fully realized through divine intervention and grace.

The truth is that individuals cannot attain the peace their hearts inherently seek without embracing the Prince of Peace, Jesus Christ, as their Savior and Lord. Authentic peace is available exclusively to those who have been reconciled to God through the transformative experience of spiritual rebirth. This reconciliation grants access to God's supernatural peace, a peace that transcends human comprehension, as articulated in Philippians 4:7-9: "And the peace of God, which surpasses all understanding, will guard your hearts and minds through Christ

Jesus." Such peace is not merely an emotional or psychological state but a profound spiritual reality, accessible only through the redemptive work of Christ and the indwelling of the Holy Spirit.

Philippians 4:7-9, *"And the peace of God, which passeth all understanding, shall keep your hearts and minds through Christ Jesus. ⁸Finally, brethren, whatsoever things are true, whatsoever things are honest, whatsoever things are just, whatsoever things are pure, whatsoever things are lovely, whatsoever things are of good report; if there be any virtue, and if there be any praise, think on these things. ⁹Those things, which ye have both learned, and received, and heard, and seen in me, do: and the God of peace shall be with you.*

Peace is one of the manifold spiritual blessings promised to believers. We are not only called to be at peace with God, through reconciliation made possible by Christ's atoning work, but also to experience the ongoing peace of God permeating our lives daily. This peace is both a relational and experiential reality for those in Christ.

As previously noted, Jesus' sacrificial death on the cross accomplished far more than the atonement for sins; it also addressed our physical and spiritual well-being. His redemptive act secured our peace, as Isaiah 53:5 declares: "The chastisement of our peace was upon Him." In this context, peace refers to a holistic state of well-being, encompassing spiritual, emotional, and even physical wholeness, which has been graciously secured by Christ's suffering on our behalf.

JEHOVAH – SHALOM "The Lord is peace" (Judges 6:24)

"No Jesus No Peace - Know Jesus Know Peace."

Chapter Three
What is this LOVE that I am Feeling?

I would like to engage in a reflection on the man from the vision, particularly the second question he posed: "What is this love that I am feeling?" By examining the Scriptures, we can gain deeper insight into what transpired in this individual's life and come to recognize that the love he experienced is accessible to all of us.

As Christians, we are endowed with the capacity to love as God loves, for "the love of God has been poured out into our hearts" (Romans 5:5). This divine love, often referred to as *agape*, represents the highest form of love, distinguished by its unfailing and unconditional nature. It transcends mere emotion, encompassing a selfless and sacrificial commitment to the well-being of others.

Romans 5:5 states, *"And hope does not put us to shame, because the love of God has been poured into our hearts through the Holy Spirit, who has been given to us."* This passage underscores that this capacity for divine love is not of human origin but is imparted to believers through the Holy Spirit.

In a world marked by division, hostility, and suffering, the need for love is undeniably profound. Love remains the essential force capable of transforming society, yet its true power can only be realized when individuals understand and practice it in the way God intended—unfailing, unconditional, and sacrificial. If people truly loved one another, societal ills such as war, crime, abuse, poverty, starvation, homelessness, and immorality would be eradicated. The man in the vision was unaware that by accepting Jesus as his Lord and Savior, he would also receive the boundless love of God.

As Christians, it is essential that we demonstrate love for those who are lost, with the aim of guiding them towards spiritual rebirth and entry into the Kingdom of God. The transformative power that can revolutionize society is the love of God, known as Agape—a selfless, unconditional love that transcends all boundaries.

In the King James Version of the Bible, the term "charity" is frequently employed as a synonym for "love." Although this term is now regarded as archaic, it essentially conveys the same concept as love. In Greek, the word translated as "charity" or "love" is "Agape," which denotes the divine, unconditional love of God.

In the English language, the term "love" is used to express a range of affections, encompassing diverse contexts and degrees of emotional attachment. For example, one might state, "I love my brother," "I love my mother," "I love my wife," "I love candy," or "I love cars." Despite the uniformity of the term, the specific context is essential for distinguishing the particular type of love being referenced.

In contrast, the Greek language employs four distinct terms to articulate various types of love, each carrying its own nuanced meaning and significance.

Storge: This term denotes an affectionate love characterized by the bonds between parents and children, as well as between loyal citizens and their rulers.

Eros: This term refers to physical or romantic love, arising from passion and desire.

Phileo: This word represents a love that cherishes and values deep personal relationships, such as the love between siblings or close friends.

All forms of love—Storge, Eros, and Phileo—should ideally be rooted in the fourth Greek term for love, Agape, which is considered the highest form of love and is frequently described as the love of God. Unlike other forms of love, Agape is not dependent on emotions or actions but represents a conscious and deliberate choice.

Agape is a selfless and sacrificial form of love that transcends conventional understanding. Unlike many forms of love that may involve seeking personal gain or recognition, Agape is distinguished by its commitment to giving without any expectation of reciprocity. Genuine Agape love is not concerned with "What will I receive?" but rather with "What can this other person gain from my love?"

In Ephesians 5:25, Paul instructs husbands to love their wives as Christ loved the Church. How did Christ love the Church? He gave Himself for it, exemplifying the essence of love as self-sacrifice. Similarly, husbands are called to embody this self-giving love.

John 3:16 provides a profound illustration of Agape love, stating: *"For God so LOVED the world, that HE GAVE his only begot Son (JESUS), that whosoever believeth in him should not perish, but have everlasting life."* (*Emphasis add*)

The concept of Agape love, often described as God's unconditional and selfless love, transcends human expectations and conditions. This form of love persists even when an individual appears resistant to being loved or when they seem undeserving of love due to their actions or words.

Agape love is not contingent upon the behavior, status, or personal attributes of the individual; it remains steadfast regardless of external factors. In the context of Agape love, personal identity, actions, or outward appearances, such as the type of clothing one wears or past behaviors, do not influence the capacity to be loved. This unconditional love is accessible to all through the power of God, affirming that every person has the potential to be embraced by God's love and receive Jesus as their Savior, irrespective of their past or present circumstances.

Agape love, characterized by its unconditional and sacrificial nature, has been a more powerful force in drawing individuals to God than any other influence. By extending genuine love and compassion and allowing others to experience the transformative nature of God's love, one can profoundly impact the lives of those around them. When an individual internalizes Agape love, it initiates a transformative process that begins internally and ultimately manifests outwardly.

This internalization of divine love enables a person to express love and forgiveness even in the face of wrongdoing. Agape love, as demonstrated by God towards humanity, extends even to those who are ungodly, showcasing its capacity to transcend human limitations and embody divine compassion and grace.

In Romans 5:6-8, 10; that's God's kind of love in action – Jesus would die for us while were yet sinners! And God loved us even when we were His enemies.

Romans 5:6-8, 10, *"For when we were yet without strength, in due time Christ died for the ungodly. [7] For scarcely for a righteous man will one die: yet peradventure for a good man some would even dare to die. [8] But God commendeth his love toward us, in that, while we were yet sinners, Christ died for us. [10] For if, when we were enemies, we were reconciled to God by the death of his Son, much more, being reconciled, we shall be saved by his life.*

Despite being unworthy of God's love, estranged from Him, and considered enemies, God still extends His love toward us. This exemplifies the profound nature of divine love, which serves as a model for how we should engage with others, including those who oppose or dislike us.

As Christians, we are called to emulate this selfless, unconditional love by showing compassion and love even towards those who harbor animosity against us. This practice not only reflects the essence of Agape love but also aligns with the fundamental Christian tenet of loving one's enemies.

GOD'S KIND OF LOVE

God's love is unwavering and unconditional, irrespective of human behavior. An examination of the Old Testament reveals how God consistently demonstrated Agape love in His dealings with the children of Israel. Despite their repeated disobedience and tendency to stray from His commandments, God's response was not one of destruction or abandonment, as a human perspective might dictate. Instead, God performed numerous miraculous acts on behalf of the Israelites.

Even when they turned away from Him, their cries for help in moments of despair were met with compassion and deliverance. This narrative underscores the profound nature of Agape love, which is characterized by forgiveness and unwavering support, even when confronted with repeated transgressions.

The children of Israel were not deserving of deliverance, yet God's immense love compelled Him to respond to the cries of His people in their moments of despair. This same divine compassion extends to us under the New Testament covenant. Our Heavenly Father provides a means for restoration through scriptures such as 1 John 1:9, which assures us that if we falter, we can seek forgiveness, and He will grant us both forgiveness and purification. This provision underscores the enduring nature of God's love, allowing for reconciliation and renewal, a testament to the unchanging and gracious character of God.

1 John 1:9, *"If we confess our sins, he is faithful and just to forgive us our sins, and to cleanse us from all unrighteousness."*

Often, our instinctive reaction when someone wrongs us is to sever ties with them. However, God commands us to respond with love toward that individual. This divine directive challenges our natural inclinations, urging us to embody a love that transcends personal grievances and reflects the unconditional nature of God's own love.

According to 1 Peter 4:8, *"And above all things have fervent charity among yourselves: for charity shall cover the multitude of sins. "*

Scripture affirms that love covers a multitude of sins, and God's love is exemplified by this principle. Therefore, if you observe your brother overtaken by a fault, the appropriate response, guided by love, is to pray for him. This reflects the essence of Agape love, which is a divine gift.

Such love can only be truly experienced by those who have a personal relationship with God, as it is imparted to us by the Holy Spirit. As stated in Romans 5:5, Agape love is shed abroad in our hearts through the Spirit of God, enabling us to love others as God loves us.

Possessing Agape love is not an automatic consequence of being a creation of God, even though all humanity is indeed created by Him. Agape love is unique to those who have become new creations in God. The prevalence of abuse, immorality, and other forms of evil is often rooted in a lack of self-respect and self-worth.

When individuals do not love themselves, they are unable to extend love to others. Without understanding or experiencing true love, people fail to value their own lives and the lives of those around them. It is only through a proper understanding of Agape love and cultivating love for oneself that one can genuinely love their neighbor.

To truly love oneself, it is essential to understand one's identity and inherent worth in Christ, as well as to grasp the depth of His love for us. According to 1 Corinthians 13:13, Agape love is the greatest virtue we can possess, surpassing all others in its significance and transformative power.

Agape love, which embodies God's own nature, is the highest and most profound aspect of life, for God Himself is love. To gain a deeper understanding of the characteristics of Agape love, one should diligently study the Word of God. By living in accordance with the light of God's Word, the Agape love that the Holy Spirit has poured into your heart will begin to guide your words and actions, shaping the way you interact with others and navigate life.

Chapter Four

The Operation of the Kingdom of God!

In John 20:19-29, the Apostle Thomas exhibits skepticism toward the testimony of his fellow apostles regarding the Resurrection of Christ. Thomas's refusal to accept their accounts without empirical evidence is notable, as he insists on physically verifying the wounds of Jesus. When Christ later appears and offers Thomas the opportunity to touch His wounds, this moment of tangible proof transforms Thomas's doubt into faith. The term "Doubting Thomas" has since emerged from this narrative, encapsulating the tension between faith and doubt within Christian belief.

This episode resonates with the contemporary Body of Christ, where many believers similarly wrestle with uncertainty about foundational doctrines. A significant portion of the Christian community appears uncertain or unaware of the tenets of their faith, reflecting a broader issue of theological illiteracy. This parallel between Thomas's doubt and modern believers' lack of doctrinal clarity highlights the enduring challenge of cultivating a fully informed and confident faith.

The prevalence of uncertainty among believers can often be attributed to a misalignment in the foundation of their belief system. Although they are identified as "believers," their faith is frequently anchored in the worldly system, governed by sensory perception and empirical evidence, rather than rooted in the divine system of faith as revealed in Scripture. This presents an important challenge: to critically evaluate one's belief system. Does it rely on the tangible and finite aspects of the world—the "five senses"—or is it founded upon God's system, which is characterized by faith and the truth of His Word?

Jesus' earthly ministry serves as a profound demonstration of a life lived in accordance with God's system of faith, in contrast to the world's system. His purpose was to model that a human being, operating through divine faith, can indeed transcend the limitations and constraints imposed by the world's system. This principle is articulated in John 8:23, where Jesus distinguishes Himself from the world's system, affirming His origin and authority as being "from above." Therefore, I encourage you to revisit these scriptures with this perspective in mind, allowing John 8:23 to illuminate the distinction between faith and the worldly system through the lens of Jesus' teachings and actions. John 8:23, *"And he said unto them, Ye are from beneath; I am from above: ye are of this world; I am not of this world.*

The Operation of the Kingdom of God

In examining Matthew 26:53, John 18:35-36, 19:10-11, and Acts 1:3, 9-11, we encounter a profound demonstration of biblical faith, the kind of faith exemplified by Jesus Christ throughout His earthly ministry. This is not merely a passive belief but an active, dynamic faith that manifests the power of God in the natural world.

The faith Jesus exhibited is the same faith that He exercised when He calmed the storm, asserting dominion over nature. It is the faith He employed when He raised the dead, demonstrating His authority over life and death. This is the faith He utilized when He healed the sick, restoring wholeness where illness prevailed. Furthermore, it is the faith with which He cast out demons, illustrating His command over the spiritual realm.

In other words, this is the kind of faith that moves the hand of God—a faith that transcends human limitations and engages with the divine. It is the faith that not only acknowledges God's power but also activates it in the world. Therefore, the faith of the Bible is not a passive acknowledgment of God's existence; it is a transformative force that aligns believers with God's will and purpose.

See these examples in Matthew 9:27-29, 14:22-31, 15:22-28; Mark 4:36-40, 5:25-34; Luke 7:1-9, 36-50.

1. We are saved through Faith: Ephesians 2:8-9.

2. The just shall live by Faith: Romans 1:17.

3. We are to fight the good fight of Faith: 1 Timothy 6:12.

4. We overcome by Faith: 1 John 5:4.

5. The only way one can please God is through Faith: Hebrews 11:6, 2 Corinthians 4:13-15, Hebrews 4:14, 10:23, and Mark 11:22-24.

What is Faith?

Hebrews 11:1 defines faith as "the substance of things hoped for, the evidence of things not seen." In this passage, faith is conceptualized as the spiritual faculty by which the heart apprehends, and lays hold of God's promises, whether these promises are conveyed through the written Word or through direct revelation. Faith, in this theological context, operates as the mechanism by which the unseen and intangible realities of God's will are made manifest in the natural realm. It functions as the bridge between divine promise and its actualization in human experience, transforming hope into reality through the assurance and unwavering conviction of God's truth.

Faith, therefore, is not merely intellectual assent but an active trust that brings the unseen into the realm of the seen, ensuring the fulfillment of God's will in the life of the believer.

In 2 Corinthians 5:7, the Apostle Paul asserts, "For we walk by faith, not by sight." Here, faith is understood as reliance on the Word of God rather than on sensory perception, highlighting a fundamental distinction between spiritual truth and the physical, sense-based world. Similarly, in John 4:24, Jesus, in His conversation with the Samaritan woman at Jacob's well, declares, "God is spirit," affirming that God exists in a spiritual realm, which transcends the tangible, material world governed by the senses.

This spiritual realm, though not perceptible to human senses, is no less real—indeed, as previously emphasized, it is more real than the temporal, physical world. The spiritual realm represents the eternal and unchanging nature of God's reality, in contrast to the fleeting and mutable nature of the sensory world. Thus, believers are called to orient their lives by faith, engaging with the unseen yet ultimate reality of God, rather than relying solely on the limitations of sensory experience.

Why more real? Because the Bible says that in the beginning God created the heavens and the earth;

so, if God, who is a spirit, created all material things, that would mean that God would have had to be in existence before He could create the material things.

Therefore, God must be more real than the things He created, as all creation is contingent upon His existence. This highlights the concept of the duality of existence, which posits that everything exists in two forms: first, in a spiritual form, beyond the realm of human physical senses, and second, in a material form, perceptible within the physical world. The spiritual form resides in the realm where God dwells, transcending the limitations of the natural world.

A vivid biblical example of this duality can be found throughout Scripture, where realities first manifest in the spiritual realm before materializing in the physical world. This illustrates that the spiritual dimension is not only foundational but also more substantial and enduring than the transient, sensory world. The duality of existence emphasizes the interdependence between the spiritual and physical, with the latter being an expression of the former.

The Operation of the Kingdom of God

According to 2 Kings 6:12-17,

> "12 and one of his servants said, "None, my lord, O king; but Elisha, the prophet who is in Israel, tells the king of Israel the words that you speak in your bedroom." 13 So he said, "Go and see where he is, that I may send and get him." And it was told him, saying, "Surely he is in Dothan." 14 Therefore he sent horses and chariots and a great army there, and they came by night and surrounded the city. 15 And when the servant of the man of God arose early and went out, there was an army, surrounding the city with horses and chariots. And his servant said to him, "Alas, my master! What shall we do?" 16 So he answered, "Do not fear, for those who are with us are more than those who are with them." 17 And Elisha prayed, and said, "LORD, I pray, open his eyes that he may see." Then the LORD opened the eyes of the young man, and he saw. And behold, the mountain was full of horses and chariots of fire all around Elisha.

According to 2 Corinthians 4:18,

> "18While we look not at the things which are seen, but at the things which are not seen: for the things which are seen are

temporal; but the things which are not seen are eternal."

Romans 12:3,

> "³For I say, through the grace given unto me, to every man that is among you, not to think of himself more highly than he ought to think; but to think soberly, according as God hath dealt to every man the measure of faith."

God's kingdom functions according to the principle of faith. To effectively engage and participate in the workings of the divine, and to bring about the manifestation of spiritual realities in the natural realm, it is essential to understand the foundational principles that govern this process. Knowledge of these spiritual laws enables believers to align themselves with the Spirit of God and operate in accordance with His Word. Only by adhering to these divine principles can one fully partake in the blessings and purposes of God's kingdom, ensuring that their actions are in harmony with God's will and His established order.

According to Mark 11:22-24;

> "²²And Jesus answering saith unto them Have faith in God ²³For verily I say unto

you, that whosoever shall say unto this mountain, Be thou removed, and be thou cast into the sea; and shall not doubt in his heart but shall believe that those things which he saith shall come to pass; he shall have whatsoever he saith. ²⁴Therefore I say unto you, what things soever ye desire, when ye pray, believe that ye receive them, and ye shall have them."

Faith, in its truest form, is the operation of God. It involves actively responding to and acting upon the Word of God. Faith is not grounded in sensory perception, philosophical reasoning, or abstract theological concepts, but rather in the authoritative truth of Scripture. Genuine faith requires a deliberate choice to trust and act upon God's Word, independent of human logic or external circumstances. It is this alignment with divine revelation, rather than reliance on worldly understanding, that defines the essence of biblical faith.

According to the Scriptures in Romans 10:9-10, salvation is attained through the belief in one's heart and the confession of one's mouth. The passage emphasizes that an individual's eternal destiny—whether in communion with God or separated from Him—is contingent upon their faith. This faith must be both internal, rooted in heartfelt conviction, and external, expressed through verbal confession.

Thus, the transformative power of salvation is not merely intellectual assent but an active, living faith that engages both the heart and the spoken word in alignment with God's promises.

In Romans 3:27, faith is described as a law, operating with the same consistency and reliability as natural laws, such as gravity. Just as the law of gravity functions regardless of one's belief in it, so too does the law of faith. It remains an unchanging principle in the spiritual realm, governing the relationship between humanity and the divine. Whether acknowledged or not, the law of faith is always at work, underscoring its foundational role in the economy of God's kingdom.

To participate in the operation of faith you must have three things:

- The Word of God (Logos/Rhema)
- A Heart that believes the Word of God (1 Peter 3:4)
- A Mouth that speaks (confesses) the Word of God (Proverb 18:21)

Below are several scriptural illustrations that elucidate the concept of faith as it operates according to the Word of God (the Bible). The fundamental principle of operating in faith involves believing in the Word of God and subsequently acting upon it. To effectively collaborate with the Spirit of God, it is imperative to understand the foundational principles that govern faith. Knowledge of these principles enables one to engage in faith-based actions in alignment with divine guidance, ensuring that one's efforts are in harmony with God's will and purpose.

Here are some examples of God operating in Faith:

- God spoke the world into existence, "Let there be light," Genesis 1:3-25.
- God change Abram's name to Abraham "Father of many nations," Genesis 17:3 -5.
- Instruction leading to the conquest of Jericho, Joshua 6:1-16, 20.
- Instruction leading to Naaman, the Syria healing, 2 King 5:1-4, 8 -14.
- God's demonstration of Peter acting on the Word of God, Luke 5:1-9; (v5).

The essence of operating in faith is to cultivate a belief in the Word of God that compels actionable responses.

True belief is evidenced by one's willingness to demonstrate faith through actions. As articulated in James 1:22, "We are not to be hearers only, but doers of the Word of God." This passage underscores that genuine faith transitions from mere intellectual assent to active implementation of God's Word. It is through the practical application of Scriptural teachings that one manifests the depth of their belief, thus moving from a state of mere belief to one of authentic faith.

Faith, as an operational principle, involves "calling those things which do not exist as though they did." This concept emphasizes speaking into reality based on the promises of God, rather than relying on visible evidence. According to 2 Corinthians 4:13 and 2 Corinthians 4:18, believers are instructed to affirm and declare the truth of God's Word rather than the observable circumstances.

In the universe, we encounter various laws, such as the law of gravity, which dictates that what goes up must come down. Similarly, the spiritual domain operates under its own law known as the Law of Faith. This principle is encapsulated in Romans 4:17, which teaches that faith involves calling things that are not as though they were.

The Law of Faith becomes accessible and effective only through the new birth experience, which aligns believers with this spiritual law. Thus, to engage with the things of God, one must operate within the framework of this law, relying on divine promises and speaking to them into existence.

In 2 Corinthians 4:13, *the Apostle Paul writes, "We having the same spirit of faith, according as it is written, I believed, and therefore have I spoken; we also believe, and therefore speak."*

This passage highlights the reciprocal relationship between belief and speech, indicating that faith is not merely a matter of internal conviction but is also expressed through verbal declarations.

However, it is important to recognize that many individuals operate in faith from a negative perspective. Instead of articulating desires aligned with God's promises, they often vocalize their fears or doubts. To effectively harness the power of faith, believers must cultivate the discipline of speaking in alignment with their aspirations and divine promises rather than merely expressing their current emotional state.

This practice of speaking what is desired in accordance with faith, rather than what is felt, is crucial for the manifestation of God's will and the transformation of one's circumstances.

Here are several examples of common negative phrases individuals often use without recognizing their detrimental impact, along with scriptural guidance for transforming these confessions into positive, faith-based affirmations:

1. "My feet are killing me."
   Scripture Reference: *1 Peter 2:24*
   "Who His own self bore our sins in His own body on the tree, that we, being dead to sins, should live unto righteousness: by whose stripes ye were healed."
   Faith Confession: "By Jesus' stripes, I am healed."
2. "I'm scared to death."
   Scripture Reference: *2 Timothy 1:7*
   "For God has not given us the spirit of fear; but of power, and of love, and of a sound mind."
   Faith Confession: "God has not given me a spirit of fear; I am empowered by His Spirit."
3. "I am broke."
   Scripture Reference: *Philippians 4:19*
   "But my God shall supply all your need according to His riches in glory by Christ

Jesus."
Faith Confession: "My God supplies all my needs according to His riches."

4. "I am so weak."
Scripture Reference: *Joel 3:10b*
"Let the weak say, 'I am strong.'"
Faith Confession: "I am strong."

5. "I am about to lose my mind."
Scripture Reference: *1 Corinthians 2:16*
"For who has known the mind of the Lord that he may instruct Him? But we have the mind of Christ."
Faith Confession: "I have the mind of Christ."

6. "I'm just dying to go."
Scripture Reference: *Proverbs 18:21*
"Death and life are in the power of the tongue, and those who love it will eat its fruit."
Faith Confession: "I speak life over myself, not death."

7. "I am catching a cold."
Scripture Reference: *1 Peter 2:24*
"Who Himself bore our sins in His own body on the tree, that we, being dead to sins, should live unto righteousness: by whose stripes ye were healed."
Faith Confession: "By Jesus' stripes, I am healed. I refuse to accept sickness."

By aligning our speech with the principles articulated in God's Word, we can effectively shape our reality and live in accordance with the divine promises of healing, strength, provision, and peace.

As believers, we are endowed with the capacity to exercise faith even in the absence of a comprehensive grasp of its underlying mechanisms. Nevertheless, the adversary often seeks to influence us towards using language and expressions that can undermine our faith, recognizing that such negative statements can adversely affect our spiritual well-being.

A clearer understanding of the operational dynamics of faith enables us to more fully receive and experience the abundant blessings that God has prepared for us. Thus, an in-depth comprehension of the principles governing faith not only enhances our ability to navigate our spiritual journey with greater efficacy but also ensures a closer alignment with the divine promises. This alignment allows us to experience the transformative power of faith in our daily lives. According to Romans 5:1-3, *"Therefore, being justified by faith, we have peace with God through our Lord Jesus Christ; ²By whom also we have access by faith into this grace wherein we stand, and rejoice in hope of the glory of God; ³And not only so, but we glory in tribulations*

Also: knowing that tribulation worketh patience." As believers, we have God's kind of faith, and we must act on it.

I trust that the biblical examples provided have elucidated the operation of faith as it pertains to divine principles. To be an effective collaborator in the work of God, it is essential to understand the foundational principles that govern faith, enabling us to align with the Spirit of God. By comprehending these ground rules, we can effectively engage with the spiritual realm and access the manifold blessings that God has prepared for us to experience during our time on earth. Faith serves as the conduit through which these blessings are received, underscoring its critical role in our spiritual journey and relationship with the divine.

Furthermore, it is crucial to recognize that faith functions as the currency of the Kingdom of God. In this divine economy, all access to, and activation of spiritual resources are mediated through faith. As articulated in Hebrews 11:6, faith is not only fundamental for engaging with the Kingdom but also essential for pleasing God. This underscores the pivotal role of faith in both accessing the benefits of the Kingdom and fulfilling our spiritual obligations.

Chapter 5
The Operations of Almighty God Yahweh's Enemy: A Biblical Examination

The Bible presents a comprehensive narrative of the struggle between good and evil, with Almighty God Yahweh on one side and His enemy, satan (or the devil), on the other. He, formerly known as lucifer, is depicted as the chief adversary of God, whose rebellion led to his downfall and subsequent enmity against the Creator's purposes. Throughout Scripture, his operations are consistently portrayed as deceptive, destructive, and diametrically opposed to the will of Yahweh. This essay explores the operations of God's enemy, as outlined in Scripture, focusing on three key aspects: deception, temptation, and destruction, with the goal of deepening our understanding of his tactics and their implications for believers today.

1. The Origin of Yahweh's Enemy: lucifer's Rebellion

The Bible introduces satan as lucifer, a high-ranking angel who became prideful and sought to usurp God's authority. In Isaiah 14:12-15, we read of Lucifer's fall: "How you have fallen from heaven, morning star, son of the dawn! ... You said in your heart, 'I will ascend to the heavens; I will raise my throne above the stars of God... I will make myself like the Most High. But you are brought down to the realm of the dead, to the depths of the pit" (NIV). This passage illustrates Lucifer's original sin—pride and self-exaltation, which ultimately led to his expulsion from heaven. His rebellion marks the beginning of enmity between him and Yahweh, setting the stage for his role as the antagonist in God's redemptive plan.

Similarly, Ezekiel 28:12-17 depicts the fall of a "cherub" who was "blameless" in his ways until wickedness was found in him. This passage, traditionally associated with lucifer, portrays his beauty, wisdom, and perfection, which were corrupted by his ambition. He is rebellion is not only against Yahweh's authority but also against His moral order, establishing the groundwork for his subsequent operations in the world.

2. Deception: The Core of satan's Operations

One of his primary operations against God's purposes is deception. From the outset, he has used lies and half-truths to distort Yahweh's word and lead humanity astray. The first instance of his deception occurs in the Garden of Eden, where he appears as a serpent to deceive Eve. Genesis 3:1-5 describes the subtlety with which he questions God's command not to eat from the tree of the knowledge of good and evil.

"Did God really say, 'You must not eat from any tree in the garden'?" (Gen. 3:1, NIV). By twisting God's words, he sows doubt and distorts the truth, leading Eve to question the goodness and integrity of Yahweh.

This pattern of deception persists throughout Scripture. Jesus refers to him as "the father of lies" in John 8:44: "He was a murderer from the beginning, not holding to the truth, for there is no truth in him. When he lies, he speaks his native language, for he is a liar and the father of lies" (NIV). His operations revolve around distorting the truth of God's word, causing people to reject Yahweh's commandments and follow paths that lead to destruction. His deception is pervasive, targeting individuals, nations, and even religious systems, as seen in 2 Corinthians 11:14, where Paul warns that "He himself masquerades as an angel of light."

3. Temptation: satan's Tool to Lead Humanity into Sin

In addition to deception, temptation is a key aspect of his operations. he seeks to entice individuals into sin, offering immediate gratification at the cost of disobedience to God. The quintessential example of how he use of temptation is found in Matthew 4:1-11, where Jesus is led into the wilderness to be tempted by the devil. He presents Jesus with three temptations, each designed to exploit human desires for power, provision, and protection. However, Jesus responds by quoting Scripture, demonstrating that reliance on God's word is the primary defense against his temptations.

This episode is significant because it highlights the nature of temptation as an attempt to undermine trust in Yahweh and promote self-reliance or disobedience. James 1:14-15 further explains the process of temptation: "But each person is tempted when they are dragged away by their own evil desire and enticed. Then, after desire has conceived, it gives birth to sin; and sin, when it is full-grown, gives birth to death" (NIV). Temptation, as orchestrated by him, is not merely an external force; it appeals to internal desires, drawing individuals away from God and into rebellion.

The temptations of satan are not limited to individual acts of sin but extend to enticing people to embrace false doctrines, ideologies, and worldviews that oppose God's truth. In 1 Timothy 4:1, Paul warns that "the Spirit clearly says that in later times some will abandon the faith and follow deceiving spirits and things taught by demons" (NIV). He operation of temptation seeks to undermine the foundation of faith itself, leading people into apostasy.

4. Destruction: The Ultimate Goal of satan's Operations.

While deception and temptation are means to an end, destruction is his ultimate goal. In John 10:10, Jesus contrasts His mission with that of satan: "The thief comes only to steal and kill and destroy; I have come that they may have life and have it to the full" (NIV). He desire is to bring ruin to God's creation, whether through physical destruction, moral corruption, or spiritual death. His enmity against Yahweh is reflected in his relentless efforts to thwart God's plan of salvation and bring harm to humanity, who bears the image of God.

The book of Job provides a vivid example of his destructive nature. In Job 1-2, his appears before God, accusing Job of serving God only because of his material blessings. With God's permission, satan is allowed to test Job, resulting in the loss of his possessions, family, and health. Although Job's faith endures, this narrative highlights his role as the "accuser" (Revelation 12:10), who seeks to inflict suffering and challenge the integrity of believers.

Moreover, he desires for destruction is ultimately aimed at leading as many people as possible into eternal separation from God.

Revelation 12:9 describes him as "the great dragon... that ancient serpent, called the devil, or satan, who leads the whole world astray" (NIV). His operations are global in scope, targeting individuals and nations in an attempt to expand his domain of darkness.

Vigilance in the Face of satan's Operations

Understanding the operations of Yahweh's enemy is crucial for believers who are called to resist his schemes and stand firm in the truth of God's word. His primary tactics—deception, temptation, and destruction—are aimed at undermining God's authority, leading people into sin, and ultimately bringing about their ruin. However, Scripture also provides the means by which believers can overcome these operations. Ephesians 6:10-18 exhorts Christians to "put on the full armor of God, so that you can take your stand against the devil's schemes" (v. 11, NIV). By relying on the truth of God's word, the righteousness of Christ, and the power of the Holy Spirit, believers can resist his attacks and remain steadfast in their faith.

In the final analysis, while his operations are formidable, they are ultimately futile in the face of God's sovereign plan of redemption. Revelation 20:10 declares he is final defeat: "And the devil, who deceived them, was thrown into the lake of burning sulfur... and will be tormented day and night for ever and ever" (NIV). The victory of Yahweh over His enemy is assured, and believers are invited to share in that victory through their faith in Christ.

Chapter Six
Two Kingdoms on one planet

One of the foundational concepts that must be grasped is the existence of two distinct kingdoms. This duality is essential for understanding the broader theological framework of the relationship between God, humanity, and creation. To fully comprehend this, it is necessary to return to the very beginning of the biblical narrative, where the principles governing these relationships are first established. The creation account in Genesis serves as the bedrock for understanding the divine order, the original intent of God for humanity, and the nature of the dominion humanity was to exercise over creation.

In Genesis 1:26-28, God declares His intention to create mankind in His image, granting them authority over the earth and its creatures. This dominion signifies humanity's role as stewards of creation, operating under the sovereign authority of God. In this original state, mankind was aligned with the Kingdom of God, characterized by righteousness, peace, and harmony between God, humanity, and the created order.

However, the introduction of sin through the fall disrupted this divine relationship and established a competing kingdom—a kingdom of rebellion and separation from God, often referred to as the "world's system" in theological discourse (cf. Genesis 3).

This fall initiated the conflict between the two kingdoms: the Kingdom of God, which is eternal and righteous, and the kingdom of this world, which is temporal and rooted in sin. The world's system operates under principles that stand in contrast to God's Kingdom, often marked by self-reliance, pride, and a pursuit of power and wealth apart from divine authority. John 18:36 echoes this dichotomy when Jesus declares, "My kingdom is not of this world" (NIV), emphasizing the fundamental difference between the spiritual reign of God and the worldly systems.

Returning to the beginning allows us to understand the origins of these two kingdoms and their respective operations. It is through this lens that the ongoing struggle between God's will and the world's system becomes clear, as well as humanity's role in choosing allegiance to one kingdom or the other.

Initially, there existed the Kingdom of Heaven, a divine realm ruled by Almighty God. In His sovereign design, God created the earth as an extension of heaven, reflecting His glory and serving as a tangible expression of His rule. The earth, often viewed as a "child" of heaven, operates in the natural realm, while the Kingdom of Heaven resides in the spiritual realm. This dual reality highlights the interplay between the spiritual and the natural, where humanity, created in God's image, possesses a unique nature—spiritual beings housed in natural bodies, intended to govern the earth under divine authority.

Within the Kingdom of Heaven, there arose a rebellion led by one of God's most exalted angels, lucifer, an anointed cherub. he is described as possessing great authority, seemingly holding a position of prominence with a form of dominion or a "throne." However, despite his elevated status, he was succumbed to pride, aspiring to elevate himself above the very Creator who fashioned him.

As Isaiah 14:13-14 recounts, his ambition was to "ascend to heaven; above the stars of God... I will make myself like the Most High" (NIV). This act of rebellion, rooted in a desire for greater power and autonomy, marked the first instance of defiance against God's divine order, leading to the introduction of conflict within the heavenly realms. He revolts not only disrupted the harmony of the spiritual realm but also laid the foundation for the cosmic struggle between good and evil that would permeate both the spiritual and natural realms.

The consequences of lucifer's rebellion were profound, resulting in his expulsion from heaven along with one-third of the angels who chose to follow him. This act of defiance led to the establishment of the kingdom of darkness, a realm characterized by opposition to God's rule and order. As a result, two distinct kingdoms now exist on one planet, each with its own governing principles and systems.

1. **The Kingdom of God**, which operates under a divine governmental structure, is founded upon laws and principles rooted in righteousness, generosity, and reciprocity. Central to this kingdom is the principle of *Giving and Receiving*, as outlined by Jesus in Matthew 4:17, where He declares the coming of the Kingdom of Heaven and calls for repentance in light of this divine reality. This system emphasizes selflessness, trust in God's provision, and living in accordance with divine law.

2. **The Kingdom of Darkness**, led by satan (formerly lucifer), operates under a corrupted governmental system. Its principles are based on *Buying and Selling*, often referred to as the Babylonian system. This structure is marked by exploitation, greed, and materialism, a stark contrast to the Kingdom of God. In Matthew 12:26,

> Jesus alludes to the disunity and dysfunction within satan's kingdom, emphasizing its inherent instability. The Babylonian system reflects a worldview dominated by self-interest, power, and control, standing in direct opposition to the divine principles of love and grace.

These two kingdoms embody the ongoing spiritual conflict that forms the foundation of the world's systems, revealing the dichotomy between divine order and rebellion. Humanity is continually confronted with a profound choice: to align with the righteous Kingdom of God, which upholds principles of justice, love, and divine governance, or to succumb to the destructive Kingdom of Darkness, characterized by corruption, self-interest, and spiritual disarray. This conflict, though spiritual in nature, has tangible implications for how individuals live, interact, and engage with the moral and ethical dimensions of the world. The decision to embrace one kingdom or the other is central to humanity's ultimate destiny and relationship with the Creator.

When God created Adam, He conferred upon him dominion over the entire earth, appointing him as its ruler or "god of this world."

This authority is clearly outlined in Genesis 1:26-28, where God declares, "Let Us make man in Our image, according to Our likeness; let them have dominion over the fish of the sea, over the birds of the air, and over the cattle, over all the earth and over every creeping thing that creeps on the earth" (NKJV). Adam was entrusted with the governance of the earth, acting as God's representative in the physical realm.

However, Adam's disobedience led to the fall of mankind. In Genesis 3:6, Adam chose to eat from the tree of the knowledge of good and evil, despite God's explicit command in Genesis 2:16-17 not to do so. This act of disobedience marked the fall, as Adam, by his choice, relinquished his God-given authority over the earth. Romans 5:12 explains the gravity of this event: "Therefore, just as through one man sin entered the world, and death through sin, and thus death spread to all men, because all sinned" (NKJV). By sinning, Adam lost the dominion he once held, and the governmental responsibility over the earth was handed over to lucifer.

lucifer, who is referred to as "the prince of the power of the air" (Ephesians 2:2, NKJV) and "the god of this world" (2 Corinthians 4:4, KJV), gained dominion over the earth through deceit. In Genesis 3:1-5, lucifer, using the serpent as his instrument, deceived Eve into disobeying God.

Through this deception, Adam and Eve's submission to his influence resulted in lucifer, now called *satan* (Revelation 12:9), taking the role of ruler over the kingdom of darkness. As Jesus later affirms, he has established a form of rule over this world: "Now is the judgment of this world; now the ruler of this world will be cast out" (John 12:31, NKJV).

Adam's disobedience, the authority and dominion that God had given to humanity were transferred to lucifer, establishing the framework for the spiritual conflict between the Kingdom of God and the kingdom of darkness. (*In this text, lowercase is used for "satan" except at the beginning of sentences.)

His objective extended beyond simply tempting Adam into disobedience; his ultimate aim was to usurp the territory—the earth—that had been entrusted to Adam, along with Adam's God-given authority. By leading Adam into sin, he successfully orchestrated Adam's abdication of his divinely ordained dominion, thereby subjecting Adam and all of humanity to satan's rule. This event catalyzed the establishment of two distinct kingdoms on earth: the Kingdom of God and the kingdom of darkness.

Initially, the Kingdom of God was the sole governing reality on earth, manifest through Adam, who was given stewardship over creation (Genesis 1:26-28). However, when Adam forfeited his authority through disobedience, the dominion he once exercised was transferred to satan, resulting in the creation of the kingdom of darkness. This shift is encapsulated in Romans 5:19, which states, "For as by one man's disobedience many were made sinners" (NKJV). Consequently, he assumed the role of ruler over this fallen world system, often referred to as "the god of this world" (2 Corinthians 4:4, NKJV).

In Genesis 3:15, God issued a prophetic promise to send a "seed" that would ultimately crush the head of satan and restore the authority of the Kingdom of God to humanity. This promised seed was none other than Jesus Christ. As John 3:16 affirms, "For God so loved the world that He gave His only begotten Son, that whoever believes in Him should not perish but have everlasting life" (NKJV). The purpose of Jesus' coming was to reestablish Heaven's governmental rule on earth through mankind, thereby reclaiming the dominion that had been forfeited by Adam.

Jesus, as the embodiment of this divine mission, came from the Kingdom of Heaven to restore the Kingdom of God on earth, even in the midst of the prevailing kingdom of darkness. His ministry was marked by the proclamation that "the kingdom of God is at hand" (Matthew 4:17, NKJV), signaling to humanity that the opportunity to realign with God's original design for earthly governance had arrived. Jesus' declaration provided the people with a choice: to embrace the Kingdom of God or to remain under the dominion of the kingdom of darkness.

However, while Jesus came to restore mankind's authority to rule over the earth, His mission did not involve the immediate destruction or eradication of the kingdom of darkness. Instead, He initiated a process of restoration, offering salvation and the opportunity for individuals to enter the Kingdom of God. As Jesus stated in John 18:36, "My kingdom is not of this world" (NKJV), emphasizing that His reign would transcend the earthly systems under satan's control. Although the kingdom of darkness continues to operate, the ultimate victory of the Kingdom of God was secured through Jesus' life, death, and resurrection, leaving the final judgment and defeat of him for a future time (Revelation 20:10).

See Matthew 4:16-17, *"The people which sat in darkness saw great light; and to them which sat in the region and shadow of death light is sprung up. From that time Jesus began to preach, and to say, Repent: for the kingdom of heaven is at hand."*

Jesus stood up in the middle of the kingdom of darkness and announced that the Kingdom of Heaven had arrived! Today, we have two kingdoms on the planet earth. So, you are either in the Kingdom of God or you are in the kingdom of darkness. It is just that simple.

Jesus understood that there are two kingdoms or government systems operating on earth. He explained that if any kingdom is divided against itself, it cannot stand, so He could not be working for satan while destroying satan. Jesus also said, *"know this: that the kingdom of heaven is come upon you."*

In other words, Jesus was explaining how you cannot operate from both kingdoms, while also declaring that the Kingdom of God had arrived. Just as Jesus understood this, we need to understand what is going on in the earth is not about people or money, it's about kingdoms and how they are governed. It's not about the Kingdom of God verses the kingdom of darkness, because the devil and all the co-horts of the kingdom of darkness have been defeated by Jesus through His death, burial and resurrection.

See Matthew 12:22-29.

> *"Then was brought unto him one possessed with a devil, blind, and dumb: and he healed him, insomuch that the blind and dumb both Spake and Saw. 23And all the people were amazed, and said, Is not this the son of David? 24 But when the Pharisees heard it, they said, this fellow doth not cast out devils, but by Beelzebub the prince of the devils. 25 And Jesus knew their thoughts, and said unto them, Every kingdom divided against itself is brought to desolation; and every city or house divided against itself shall not stand: 26 And if satan cast out satan, he is divided against himself; how shall then his kingdom stand? 27 And if I by Beelzebub cast out devils, by whom do your children cast them out? therefore they shall be your judges. 28 But if I cast out devils by the Spirit of God, then the kingdom of God is come unto you. 29 Or else how can one enter into a strong man's house, and spoil his goods, except he first bind the strong man? and then he will spoil his house.*

As the governing body of Christ, the churches are the called-out ones, (Greek word Ecclesia) we have executive leaders as Apostles, Prophets, Evangelists, Pastors and Teachers. These leaders receive instruction from headquarters, where the Lord Jesus Christ is seated at the right-hand of the throne of God in Heaven via the Holy Spirit.

The executive leaders then impart revelation knowledge received from Heaven to the citizens of the Kingdom of Heaven and confirm what individual have received via the Holy Spirit. This impartation and confirmation help us to be effective citizens of the Kingdom of God.

As members of the body of Christ, citizens of the kingdom of Heaven, the citizens come together for church service to receive instructions about Kingdom operations. As ambassadors of the Kingdom of God these instructions are disseminated to each jurisdiction as to how to be effective Christians living in the Kingdom of God. This is similar to the government in the United States. We have various executive leaders, elected officials in the federal government that provide the laws for state officials to extend to individual localities. As United States citizens we are to be informed citizens and to help others to follow the law.

As a Christian, we are citizens of the Kingdom of God according to Colossian 1:9 -13. As a child of God, we have been translated from the kingdom of darkness into the kingdom of God through being born-again. It's about which kingdom you are in and whose government you will follow?

To become a citizen of Kingdom of God, you first must be born- again, and then you have to learn how to live by the laws and principles established by the Kingdom of God in order to become an effective citizen of the Kingdom of God.

You must obey the "constitution" or the terms of the Holy Bible for citizenship. The bible says in *John 3* that *"you must be born again"* to enter the Kingdom of God. The only way go get into the kingdom of God and to be a partaker of the kingdom of Heaven's lifestyle is to be born-again, or to be born from above.

When the Bible says we must be born again, in the original Greek it says we must be born from above. We are actually born from heaven another government, another country the kingdom of God. Today, through the body of Christ, the Holy Spirit can saturate the whole earth. When the Holy Spirit came into the earth after Jesus' ascension, He set up residence inside of every believer.

Once we are born again, the Comforter lives inside us. *We come into the kingdom of God, and at the same time the kingdom of God comes inside of us.* As believers, we have the whole kingdom of God inside of us.

In the kingdom God has provided everything we need here on earth understanding, wisdom, peace, joy, health, prosperity, provision, and protection. The Holy Spirit is within us to help us access every natural and supernatural thing we need.

If the kingdom of God is inside of us, then we don't need to worry about anything. God has already provided everything. God's protection is one provision of the kingdom that is inside of us. We can't see the kingdom; however, we can see the results of it. Jesus said,

Matthew 6:25, 32-34, "The kingdom of God cometh not with observation: The kingdom of God is a spiritual reality and is more real than anything we can see with our physical eyes. When we receive Jesus, we receive it all. We have a spiritual fountain inside, and we will never thirst again.

John 4:13, *"We will never have to go to another source to provide for us."*

Everything we need is inside of us. God will bring to us, lead us to, and create for us everything that we need in this earth, independent of what's going on around us.

Now that we have established the existence of these two kingdoms, how do they operate? The Kingdom of Heaven, where God operates by faith

and is where God deals with us through our born-again spirit, according to Proverb 20:27.
"The spirit of man is the candle of the LORD, searching all the inward parts of the belly."

For clarity let me explain the makeup of mankind in the next chapter.

Chapter Seven

The Three-fold Nature of Man: Spirit, Soul, and Body

We are called to view ourselves according to the truths revealed in Scripture. The Bible teaches that we are fundamentally spiritual beings, possessing a soul and residing in a physical body. My spirit is the part of my being that was born again, the place where God dwells within me (John 3:6). As such, I carry the nature of God within me, and it is this spiritual nature that compels me toward righteousness.

I. The First Dimension of Man – The Spirit

Humanity's primary and most essential dimension is the spirit, the part of us that connects directly with God. In essence, we are spirit beings, created in the image of God, who is Himself a spirit (John 4:24). God designed humankind with the capacity for fellowship with Him, enabling us to know Him intimately. This spiritual nature places humanity in a unique class of being, distinguished by our ability to commune with God on a spiritual level.

The distinction between the threefold nature of man—spirit, soul, and body—is clearly articulated in Scripture. Hebrews 4:12 speaks of the Word of God as "living and active, sharper than any two-edged sword, piercing to the division of soul and spirit, of joints and marrow" (ESV), demonstrating that our spiritual nature can be distinguished from the physical and mental aspects of our being. 1 Thessalonians 5:23 further emphasizes this trichotomy, praying that "the whole spirit, soul, and body be preserved blameless at the coming of our Lord Jesus Christ" (NKJV).

The rebirth of the human spirit is central to the Christian experience, as described in John 3:7, where Jesus teaches the necessity of being "born again" to enter the Kingdom of God. This regeneration of the spirit aligns us with God's nature and restores our ability to fellowship with Him. Romans 2:28-29 underscores the significance of the spirit in defining the true nature of a person, asserting that "a person is not a Jew who is one only outwardly... but one inwardly, and circumcision is a matter of the heart, by the Spirit" (ESV). The spirit, therefore, is the very heart of man, the innermost part where God's transformative work takes place.

In 1 Corinthians 14:14, the apostle Paul affirms the active role of the spirit in prayer: "For if I pray in a tongue, my spirit prays, but my mind is unfruitful" (NIV). This passage highlights the primacy of the spirit in communicating with God, often transcending human understanding. Furthermore, in 2 Kings 6:17, the Lord opened the servant's spiritual eyes, enabling him to see beyond the natural realm and perceive the spiritual forces at work, demonstrating that the spirit is capable of perceiving realities that the natural mind cannot.

Ultimately, the spirit is the dimension of man through which we know God, communicate with Him, and experience His presence. Our spiritual nature defines our true identity, setting us apart as beings created for fellowship with the Divine.

God created humanity for His own pleasure and purpose, distinguishing humans from animals through their unique capacity for spiritual fellowship with Him. Unlike animals, which are driven by instinct and physical needs, humans are endowed with a spiritual nature that allows for a relationship with the Divine. To facilitate this relationship, humanity must exist in the same spiritual category as God. As affirmed in John 4:24, "God is Spirit, and those who worship Him must worship in spirit and truth" (NKJV), indicating that our engagement with God must be through our own spirit.

Since God is a Spirit, He cannot be known or interacted with through physical or mental means alone. Our knowledge of and communion with God are therefore spiritual in nature. This spiritual dimension is crucial because, despite God's nature as Spirit, He chose to manifest Himself in the physical realm through Jesus Christ. This incarnation is described in John 1:1-3,

14: "In the beginning was the Word, and the Word was with God, and the Word was God... And the Word became flesh and dwelt among us" (NKJV). This passage emphasizes that Jesus, while being fully divine, took on human form to bridge the gap between humanity and God.

Additionally, Luke 16:19-31, which recounts the story of Lazarus and the rich man, illustrates the reality of spiritual existence and the afterlife, underscoring the separation between physical and spiritual realms. Furthermore, Ezekiel 36:26-27 promises a transformative new heart for God's people: "I will give you a new heart and put a new spirit within you" (NIV). This promise highlights the importance of spiritual renewal in establishing a relationship with God.

2 Corinthians 5:17-21 and 2 Corinthians 5:6-8 further elaborate on this transformation. In 2 Corinthians 5:17, Paul states, "Therefore, if anyone is in Christ, he is a new creation; old things have passed away; behold, all things have become new" (NKJV), signifying the profound change that occurs within a person who is spiritually reborn. Similarly, 2 Corinthians 5:6-8 discusses the confidence and hope believers have in their spiritual transformation and future with God: "So we are always confident, knowing that while we are at home in the body, we are absent from the Lord. For we walk by faith, not by sight" (NKJV).

Humanity's spiritual nature aligns with God's essence as Spirit, enabling a genuine fellowship that transcends physical and mental realms. The incarnation of Jesus as fully God and fully man bridges the gap between humanity and divinity, providing the means for spiritual renewal and communion with God.

Residing in the natural, physical world, it can be challenging to grasp the reality that the spiritual realm is more fundamental than our material existence. Many people conceptualize their existence solely in terms of their physical bodies, believing that death equates to the end of their existence. However, biblical teachings reveal that the true essence of humanity is the inward man — the hidden person of the heart, who is an eternal being. This perspective is supported by Scriptures indicating that while our physical bodies will eventually return to dust, our spiritual selves persist beyond physical death (2 Corinthians 4:16-18).

The inward man, or spirit, represents our true self, which endures eternally. As articulated in 2 Corinthians 4:16-18, "Therefore we do not lose heart. Though outwardly we are wasting away, yet inwardly we are being renewed day by day. For our light and momentary troubles are achieving for us an eternal glory that far outweighs them all. So, we fix our eyes not on

The Three-fold Nature of Man

what is seen, but on what is unseen, since what is seen is temporary, but what is unseen is eternal" (NIV). This passage underscores the distinction between our transient physical existence and our eternal spiritual nature.

Moreover, our spirit possesses a voice, often referred to as our 'conscience.' This inner voice plays a critical role in moral decision-making and spiritual guidance. As we align our lives with the Word of God, it is through our spirit that God communicates, leads, guides, and directs us. This dynamic is supported by the teachings of Scripture, which emphasize the importance of spiritual discernment and the role of the inner man in understanding and following God's will.

The spiritual realm represents a deeper and more enduring reality than the physical world we experience. Our true essence is the eternal inward man, and our spirit, through its voice of conscience, interacts with divine guidance as we walk in accordance with God's Word.

II. Man's Second Dimension - The Soul

In examining the second aspect of humanity's threefold nature, we turn our attention to the soul. The soul encompasses the dimensions of emotion, cognition, and will, and is integral to our mental and reasoning processes.

Romans 12:2 provides insight into the role of the soul in the process of transformation: "And do not be conformed to this world, but be transformed by the renewing of your mind, that you may prove what is that good and acceptable and perfect will of God" (NKJV). This passage indicates that while God engages with our spirit to effect spiritual renewal, the responsibility for renewing our mind—an aspect of the soul—rests with us. The transformation of the mind is crucial for aligning with God's will and embracing our new identity in Christ.

The battleground for the Christian often resides in the mind, which is part of the soulish dimension. It is in this realm that choices are made and where the enemy may seek to disrupt our alignment with divine purposes. Reason, as the voice of the soul, plays a pivotal role in decision-making. Without vigilance, we can rationalize ourselves away from God's will, as our reasoning can lead us astray if not anchored in divine truth.

Scripture acknowledges the importance of reasoning and reflection in the spiritual journey. For instance, Isaiah 1:18 invites us to "come now, and let us reason together," emphasizing the role of thoughtful engagement in understanding and following God's directives.

Initially, after conversion, the flesh may exert a predominant influence, but as spiritual growth progresses, the spirit increasingly guides and influences our decisions. The mind or soul occupies a critical position, acting as the decision-making interface between the flesh and the spirit.

The ongoing spiritual journey involves a process where the spirit, empowered by God's grace, gradually exerts greater influence over the soul, leading to a more profound alignment with God's will.

The soul, comprising our emotions, intellect, and will, is central to our spiritual and moral decision-making. While God interacts with our spirit to effect transformation, the renewal of the mind remains a personal responsibility, crucial for navigating the spiritual and moral challenges of life.

Our decisions and choices are pivotal in shaping our lives. As autonomous beings, we determine what actions we will take and what behaviors we will adopt. This underscores the necessity of immersing our minds in the Word of God. To "restore our souls," we must ensure that our understanding is grounded in biblical principles. Without this foundation, our minds are prone to align with fleshly desires rather than divine will.

By embedding the Word of God into our minds, we effectively counteract influences that oppose God's intentions.

We should affirm the truth of our identity and transformation: "I am a spirit, I have a soul, and I live in a physical body. My mind is renewed, and my body is subdued." This declaration aligns with Paul's instruction, which emphasizes the importance of engaging both our bodies and minds in the process of spiritual renewal:

Engage the Body: Paul exhorts believers to "present your bodies a living sacrifice" (Romans 12:1, NKJV), highlighting the need for physical dedication to God's service.

Renew the Mind: Paul also instructs, "be transformed by the renewing of your mind" (Romans 12:2, NKJV). This transformation involves a continuous process of mind renewal through the intake of God's Word. God has provided His Word as a primary means for this renewal, allowing individuals to study and meditate on Scripture in their private devotion. Additionally, the church plays a crucial role in this process by providing anointed teachers who impart deeper understanding and revelation of the Kingdom of God. According to James 1:21, "Receive with meekness the implanted word, which is able to save your souls" (NKJV), and

Psalm 23:3 states, "He restores my soul; He leads me in the paths of righteousness for His name's sake" (NKJV). These passages emphasize the dual approach to mind renewal: personal study and meditation on the Word, alongside instruction from divinely appointed teachers.

Renewing the mind involves actively engaging with Scripture both individually and communally. By feeding upon God's Word and receiving teaching from anointed leaders, believers can strengthen their understanding and align their lives more fully with divine principles, thereby walking in the light of God's truth.

III. Man's Third Dimension - The Body

In exploring the third dimension of humanity's nature—the body—it is essential to understand its role and function from a biblical perspective. While the spirit represents the inward man, the body constitutes the outward man, serving as the physical vessel in which we reside during our earthly life. The body possesses its own form of expression, referred to as 'feeling.' This physical aspect is often described as the 'suit' or 'house' we inhabit on earth. However, reliance on our feelings can lead to spiritual peril, as suggested by 2 Corinthians 4:4, which describes Satan as "the god of this world" (NKJV).

If we allow our bodies and their sensations to dominate our decisions, we risk permitting the influence of Satan to penetrate our lives. It is crucial, regardless of our personal feelings, to adhere to the directives provided in God's Word.

The body itself is not inherently evil, but it can be used for unrighteous purposes if not properly managed. We are entrusted with the responsibility of controlling our bodies. If we permit our bodies to dictate our actions, we are yielding to the flesh, which encompasses various aspects of the sinful nature: the lower nature, the old nature, the selfish nature, the carnal nature, and the old self. In essence, the flesh represents the sinful desires or impulses that can arise in both saved and unsaved individuals.

Contrary to the notion that the flesh is uncontrollable, Romans 6:14 asserts that "sin shall not have dominion over you" (NKJV). Through Jesus' sacrifice on the cross, believers are empowered to overcome the dominion of sin.

Galatians 2:20 further underscores this transformative process: "I have been crucified with Christ; it is no longer I who live, but Christ lives in me" (NKJV). This passage highlights the necessity of spiritually identifying with Christ's crucifixion to achieve victory over the flesh.

1 Corinthians 9:27 illustrates the necessity of self-discipline: "But I discipline my body and bring it into subjection" (NKJV). This verse emphasizes that controlling the body is a deliberate choice.

While we can allow the body to continue in its previous patterns of behavior, we also have the option to exercise control over it. By doing so, we align with our inward man and offer our bodies as "a living sacrifice" to God, as instructed in Romans 12:1: "I urge you, brethren, by the mercies of God, to present your bodies a living sacrifice, holy, acceptable to God" (NKJV).

Ultimately, the management of our bodies is our responsibility. Romans 1:17 indicates that Paul's instructions are directed toward believers, not sinners, reinforcing that the call to present our bodies as living sacrifices is a continual imperative for those who are already in Christ. The choice remains ours: to either let our bodies dictate our actions or to control them and present them for divine purposes.

According to 2 Corinthians 5:17; the body is not new; however, at the coming of Christ we will have a new body. Right now, God expects us to do something with our bodies.

As we have examined from the Scriptures regarding the tripartite nature of humanity, it becomes evident that we hold the power of decision-making in our lives. We are responsible for choosing our actions and aligning them with divine principles. It is incumbent upon us to allow Christ to exercise His lordship in our lives, leading us to victory and ensuring that we are overcomers and spirit-led believers in every aspect of our existence. Amen.

According to Galatians 5:22-23, the characteristics of a life led by the Spirit should be evident in our behavior. These attributes—love, joy, peace, longsuffering, gentleness, goodness, faith, meekness, and temperance—reflect the principles and guidelines of the Kingdom of God. They serve as indicators of our alignment with divine standards and our adherence to spiritual guidance.

In contrast, Galatians 5:19-21 highlights the nature of the world's kingdom, which is influenced by the lusts of the flesh. This passage details behaviors and desires that are contrary to the Kingdom of God, emphasizing the contrast between living according to the flesh and living according to the Spirit. Therefore, our choices should reflect a commitment to kingdom principles, manifesting the fruit of the Spirit in our daily lives while resisting the temptations and influences that seek to lead us astray.

For everything that God has, Satan has a counterfeit, or he has perverted what God has created. Now we can understand what Paul was saying in writing to the Galatians in 5:16-25.

Galatians in 5:16-25. *"This I say then, Walk in the Spirit, and ye shall not fulfill the lust of the flesh. 17 For the flesh lusteth against the Spirit, and the Spirit against the flesh: and these are contrary the one to the other: so that ye cannot do the things that ye would. 18 But if ye be led of the Spirit, ye are not under the law. 19 Now the works of the flesh are manifest, which are these; Adultery, fornication, uncleanness, lasciviousness, 20 Idolatry, witchcraft, hatred, variance, emulations, wrath, strife, seditions, heresies, 21 Envyings, murders, drunkenness, revellings, and such like: of the which I tell you before, as I have also told you in time past, that they which do such things shall not inherit the kingdom of God. 22 But the fruit of the Spirit is love, joy, peace, longsuffering, gentleness, goodness, faith.*

In Galatians 5:22-23, the Apostle Paul delineates the attributes that should characterize the life of one who is walking in the Spirit. These virtues — love, joy, peace, longsuffering, gentleness, goodness, faith, meekness, and temperance — serve as indicators of adherence to the principles and guidelines of the Kingdom of God. They reflect the transformative impact of the Spirit's influence on an individual's conduct and character.

Conversely, Galatians 5:19-21 describes the behaviors associated with the kingdom of this world and the influence of Satan, which operate through the lusts of the flesh. This passage enumerates the manifestations of living according to the flesh, contrasting sharply with the fruit of the Spirit. It underscores the distinction between the principles governing the Kingdom of God and those that govern the natural, worldly system, which is driven by sinful desires and actions.

Chapter Eight
Faithfulness, Consistency, Diligence and Excellence

In the following chapters, I will present the essential steps required for attaining spiritual maturity. Central to this process are four foundational concepts: Faithfulness, Consistency, Diligence, and Excellence. It is critical that we develop a comprehensive understanding of these terms and actively integrate them into our daily spiritual practices. The life that God intends for us demands a thoughtful and deliberate effort, underscoring the need for intentional growth and disciplined application. Spiritual maturity, as a divine aspiration, does not materialize without the alignment of our actions with these key principles.

Psalms 106:3 says, "Blessed are they who maintain justice, who <u>constantly</u> do what is right" (NIV).

The Imperative of Faithfulness – "A faithful person consistently pursues righteousness, even when immediate results are not apparent." Several years ago, I embarked on a small gardening project on my back deck. In that initial year, my efforts yielded a modest harvest, including peppers, cucumbers, and tomatoes, all cultivated from seeds and plants sown earlier in the spring. However, my inexperience with gardening presented certain challenges. I was unaware of the importance of using nutrient-rich, fertile soil, the strategies necessary to protect the garden from pests and wildlife, and the critical role of consistent watering. These lessons, learned through trial and error, serve as a powerful metaphor for faithfulness, emphasizing the necessity of sustained, informed effort to achieve long-term success.

The following year my crop was a much better crop and consisted of: Green peppers, cucumbers, tomatoes, cantaloupes, and watermelons.

The Importance of Consistency – Initially, I procured organic topsoil from the local hardware store, supplemented it with horse manure, and planted the seeds and seedlings at the appropriate time. I ensured the garden was watered consistently, adhering to a regular schedule. These seemingly minor adjustments, coupled with a commitment to faithfulness and consistency in executing each task correctly, resulted in a significantly larger harvest than the previous year. Consistent watering was especially crucial, as water is an essential element for a garden to yield the desired outcome.

This illustrates that consistent effort, much like in spiritual growth, is fundamental to achieving optimal results.

The Necessity of Diligence – While many individuals equate success with the attainment of wealth or social standing, the most profound form of success is spiritual success, which fosters a deeper relationship with God. True success is measured by our growth in the grace and knowledge of our Lord Jesus Christ, as emphasized in 2 Peter 3:18. Spiritual growth is not a passive process but requires deliberate effort and diligence. A foundational guide to this process can be found in 2 Peter 1:5-11, where the apostle outlines the steps necessary for cultivating a life of spiritual maturity and divine fulfillment. Through diligent pursuit of these virtues, one experiences the highest form of success: closeness to God.

The Apostle Peter exhorts believers to "give all diligence," which implies acting with intense zeal and exerting considerable effort to cultivate specific virtues. This call to earnest and deliberate action underscores the necessity of consciously striving to develop these attributes in our lives. Spiritual growth in Christ is neither instantaneous nor accidental; it is a process that demands time, patience, and disciplined labor.

Moreover, in 2 Peter 1:5, Peter emphasizes the need to "add" each virtue in succession, suggesting that these qualities must be cultivated in harmony with one another to achieve a holistic transformation. This progressive development of virtues indicates an interconnected relationship, where each virtue complements and strengthens the others, ultimately contributing to spiritual maturity and alignment with God's purpose.

The development of these virtues must occur in conjunction with one another; we cannot selectively cultivate those we prefer while neglecting others. Many Christians remain spiritually immature, and some even fall away, because they fail to fortify their faith by actively incorporating these virtues into their lives. While some may have been devoted followers of God for many years, without continual growth, they are merely repeating the same foundational stage year after year. True spiritual maturity requires ongoing development, a dynamic process that moves beyond initial faith and strives toward the fullness of life in Christ.

The Necessity of Excellence – It is both unbiblical and dishonorable for Christians to settle for mediocrity by adopting a lukewarm, lazy, careless, or undisciplined approach to their faith.

Such an attitude stands in direct contradiction to the example of Christ. He gave Himself for the purpose of redeeming us from all lawlessness and purifying for Himself a people uniquely His own, zealous for good works (Titus 2:14).

This call to excellence is intrinsic to the Christian life, as it reflects the transformative power of Christ's sacrifice and the high standard to which we are called in our pursuit of holiness and good deeds. Anything less diminishes the profound significance of His redemptive work.

Mediocrity prioritizes self-satisfaction or the approval of others over the pursuit of pleasing God. It leads to minimal growth in grace and yields little substantive progress in the pursuit of true godliness. A mediocre faith engages in prayer merely to soothe the conscience but lacks the depth necessary to foster Christlikeness. It desires faith without the corresponding faithfulness, performing religious acts devoid of genuine connection with the Master. Mediocrity seeks Jesus as Savior, yet resists submitting to Him as Lord. While a mediocre faith may deceive others, it cannot deceive God. True faith requires full-hearted devotion, not the half measures of spiritual complacency.

What is excellence? Excellence is the pursuit of doing all things with the utmost care and quality, exemplified by Jesus Christ. In Mark 7:37, after witnessing His miracles and observing His way of life, the people concluded, "He has done all things well." Excellence, therefore, is not merely an action but a spirit—just as mediocrity is a spirit. The spirit of excellence is imparted to believers when they accept Jesus as both Lord and Savior. It reflects Christ's character, calling us to a standard of living that honors God through diligence, integrity, and wholehearted devotion in all things.

Living outside of a relationship with Jesus Christ is the embodiment of mediocrity, for it lacks the transformative power and purpose found in Him. In contrast, excellence is defined by absolute dependence and unwavering trust in God. Caleb, in his bold declaration, exemplified this spirit of excellence, proclaiming that the Israelites were "well able" to claim their inheritance because God was with them (Numbers 13:30). As Caleb stilled the people and confidently urged them to seize their promise, his faith reflected the assurance that success comes through divine strength.

This truth is further echoed in 1 John 4:4, which reminds us that "greater is He that is in you, than he that is in the world."

Faithfulness, Consistency, Diligence and Excellence

True excellence arises from recognizing and living in the power of God's presence, enabling believers to overcome obstacles and fulfill their divine calling.

Those who doubted God's promises were exemplifying mediocrity in their response to divine assurance. God desires that His children embody His nature in all aspects of their lives. The spirit of excellence is not an automatic endowment but a pursuit that must be actively sought. As indicated in 2 Corinthians 3:18, "But we all, with unveiled face, beholding as in a mirror the glory of the Lord, are being transformed into the same image from glory to glory, just as by the Spirit of the Lord." This passage highlights that transformation into excellence is a gradual process, reflecting God's glory through continual spiritual growth.

To cultivate excellence, one must remain steadfast in engaging with God's Word. It is through Scripture that the spirit of excellence is imparted. Romans 12:1-2 underscores this imperative: "I beseech you therefore, brethren, by the mercies of God, that you present your bodies a living sacrifice, holy, acceptable to God, which is your reasonable service. And do not be conformed to this world, but be transformed by the renewing of your mind, that you may prove what is that good and acceptable and perfect will of God."

The directive to renew the mind and avoid conformity to worldly standards is essential for attracting and embodying excellence, as it aligns believers with the divine will and standards. Examine the terminology used in the Scripture: it instructs us not to be conformed but to be transformed, emphasizing that this transformation is an ongoing process.

God desires that His people distinguish themselves in all their endeavors, refusing to yield to the mediocrity that pervades the surrounding environment. The influence of the world, governed by the devil, often seeks to propagate mediocrity in the lives of believers.

John 10:10 highlights this contrast: "The thief comes only to steal, and to kill, and to destroy; I have come that they may have life, and that they may have it more abundantly." This passage underscores that while the adversary aims to undermine and diminish, Christ's mission is to provide abundant life, characterized by excellence. An excellent mindset does not destroy but seeks to rectify and improve. Therefore, believers are called to oppose everything associated with mediocrity. The realization of excellence is attainable, provided one maintains the conviction that it is indeed possible.

The Bible asserts that nothing is impossible for those who are children of God. Believers are encouraged to adopt a mindset that aligns with this divine assurance, understanding that whatever God places in their hearts is achievable. Proverbs 23:7 states, "For as he thinks in his heart, so is he." This verse underscores the profound impact that one's thoughts have on actions; therefore, cultivating a mindset of excellence is crucial.

Excellence should be reflected not only in spiritual pursuits but in every aspect of life. This includes one's personal relationships, marriages, professional endeavors, and daily decision-making. To embody excellence in all these areas, believers must consistently apply their faith and principles, thereby demonstrating a holistic commitment to high standards in every dimension of their existence.

Chapter Nine
Introduction to Spiritual Maturity

One of the primary concerns for new parents is ensuring the normal and healthy development of their newborn. Physicians meticulously track growth metrics, such as weight gain, to ensure that the child follows expected patterns. When deviations occur, doctors investigate to identify and address any underlying issues. Similarly, the maturity of their children is a significant concern for parents. In a parallel manner, our Heavenly Father is deeply invested in the spiritual maturation of His children. He expects each believer to progress towards a level of maturity commensurate with that of fully developed, active participants in His kingdom. Just as pediatric growth is carefully monitored, so too is our spiritual growth expected to meet the standards set by God for His children.

Spiritual Maturity as a Process

Spiritual maturity is a progressive journey that commences with an individual's acceptance of Jesus Christ as Lord and Savior, resulting in a spiritual rebirth. The goal of this process is to attain a comprehensive understanding of one's nature: recognizing oneself as a spirit with a soul residing within a physical body.

Spiritual maturity involves allowing our spirit to assume its rightful role as sovereign, our soul to function as a servant, and our body to serve as an instrument. This hierarchical alignment is crucial for achieving spiritual growth. As discussed in a preceding chapter, understanding human composition is essential, and recognizing the presence of the Holy Spirit within our spirits is fundamental. 1 John 4:4 affirms this, stating, "Greater is He that is in you than he that is in the world."

The Old Testament provides an illustrative example to elucidate this concept. In the Book of Exodus, for instance, we observe the construction of the Tabernacle. The Tabernacle was a sacred structure designed specifically for the worship of God.

It was constructed with three distinct areas: the outer court, the inner court, and the Holy of Holies. The outer court served as the initial area of access, where sacrifices and offerings were made. The inner court, or the Holy Place, was where the priests performed their duties and where the altar of incense was located. The Holy of Holies, the innermost and most sacred space, housed the Ark of the Covenant and represented the direct presence of God.

Each level of the Tabernacle symbolizes a deeper degree of spiritual engagement, reflecting the process of entering into a closer relationship with the divine.

Our bodies can be likened to the outer court, our souls to the inner court, and our spirits to the Holy of Holies within the Tabernacle. It is crucial to recognize that spiritual maturation is a gradual process. In contemporary society, where instant gratification is often emphasized, there is a prevailing expectation for immediate results. This cultural tendency frequently overlooks the importance of a methodical process. For instance, consider the restoration of damaged drywall. Recently, a minor kitchen fire led to damage in the wall due to the actions of a young, enthusiastic firefighter.

I hired a contractor to repair the damage, and he outlined the process as follows:

Initial Removal: The first step involves cutting out the damaged section of the drywall.

Replacement: The next step is to replace the removed drywall with new material, securing it with drywall nails, tape, and compound.

Sanding and Smoothing: After allowing the compound to dry, which typically takes several hours, the area must be sanded.

Additional compound may be applied as needed, followed by further sanding to achieve a smooth finish.

Painting: The final steps include applying a primer coat, allowing it to dry, and then adding a finishing coat of paint, which also requires time to dry.

This methodical approach illustrates that restoration and improvement, whether in physical repairs or spiritual growth, necessitate patience and a commitment to the process.

The restoration process for damaged drywall, which can span several days, serves as a useful analogy for spiritual maturation. This process is neither instant nor immediate; rather, it unfolds over time. Similarly, spiritual growth does not occur overnight. It is a gradual process, the duration of which can be influenced by one's diligence and commitment to excellence.

Our compassionate Heavenly Father, in His wisdom, has provided a plan for spiritual maturity within His Holy Word. This plan is designed to guide believers towards a state where their response to the Holy Spirit is immediate and unimpeded by the soul (comprising the mind, will, and emotions) or the body (encompassing feelings, flesh, and sensory perceptions).

Achieving this level of spiritual maturity requires a consistent effort to align one's actions with the guidance of the Holy Spirit, ensuring that spiritual growth progresses in accordance with divine expectations.

A life that is fully submitted to the Lord and guided by the leadership of the Holy Spirit will markedly differ from one influenced by the corruption of this world. Spiritual development mirrors the progression of physical life, encompassing three distinct stages that correspond to childhood, youth, and adulthood.

1. The Stage of Spiritual Childhood

Spiritual childhood represents the initial phase of a Christian's journey, occurring shortly after they have accepted Jesus Christ as their personal Lord and Savior. At this stage, new believers are still acclimating to the profound reality that their sins are forgiven, and they have been delivered from judgment and eternal separation from God. Much like physical infants, baby Christians are dependent on others for spiritual nourishment and guidance.

They require support to navigate their new faith, as they lack the experience and understanding necessary to independently live out their Christian life.

2. Becoming a Spiritual Young Person

The transition to spiritual adolescence or young adulthood encompasses the period from late teenage years into early adulthood. This stage is characterized by a period of conflict and the development of spiritual strength. Believers in this phase confront the realities of Christian living and engage in spiritual warfare against the adversary. It is during these years that individuals begin to effectively wield the "sword of the Spirit," which is the Word of God, to counteract the attacks of the enemy and fortify their faith. This stage marks a critical development of spiritual resilience and proficiency in using scriptural tools to combat spiritual challenges.

3. Becoming a Mature Adult

A mature believer has cultivated an intimate relationship with God that has developed over an extended period. This depth of knowledge is acquired through enduring spiritual growth and overcoming challenges, including victories over spiritual adversaries. The mature Christian's life exhibits a profound quality that is achieved through consistently applying the Word of God in various circumstances.

The essence of knowing God intimately is characterized by a heightened sensitivity to the guidance of the Holy Spirit, allowing one to perceive divine direction that may be missed by others. This level of spiritual intimacy is evidenced by an ability to discern and follow the Spirit's leading with precision and depth.

In 2 Peter 1:5-7, the Apostle Peter employs the metaphor of a staircase to illustrate the progression from one stage of spiritual development to another. He outlines eight virtues that should be evident in the life of a believer who is truly committed to their faith:
- (1) **Virtue:** Moral excellence and integrity.
- (2) **Knowledge:** Understanding and insight.
- (3) **Temperance:** Self-control and moderation.
- (4) **Patience:** Endurance and perseverance.
- (5) **Godliness:** Reverence and piety.
- (6) **Brotherly Kindness:** Affection and compassion towards others.
- (7) **Charity:** Unconditional love and benevolence.

Peter's exhortation is clear: to affirm one's calling, these virtues must be actively cultivated. If these qualities are not apparent in a believer's life, their profession of faith may be called into question.

This passage underscores that spiritual maturity is an ongoing process, involving the deliberate and sustained effort to advance through these stages of relational development and virtue.

By consistently applying the eight virtues outlined in 2 Peter 1:5-7 and integrating them into daily life, individuals can transform their character from one reflective of worldly corruption to one embodying the divine nature of God. This transformative process requires a dedicated commitment to two critical principles: diligence and excellence.

Diligence, as emphasized in the Scriptures, involves a persistent and earnest effort in pursuing spiritual growth. Excellence reflects the high standards to which believers are called to adhere in their daily lives. These principles must be comprehensively understood and diligently practiced achieving spiritual maturity.

As stated in 2 Peter 1:1-10, the Bible asserts that grace and peace are multiplied through the knowledge of God. Furthermore, God has provided everything necessary for life and godliness through this knowledge, underscoring the importance of diligence in spiritual development.

The integration of these virtues, coupled with a commitment to diligence and excellence, is essential for advancing in spiritual maturity and reflecting the divine nature of God.

Let's now define some of the key concepts from the passage in 2 Peter 1:5-7:

Faith: This is the initial entry point into God's family and serves as the foundational element upon which a Christian's life should be built. It is through faith that believers establish their relationship with God and begin their spiritual journey.

Virtue: Virtue acts as a safeguard against the entrapments of sin. For Christians, virtues are derived from biblical teachings and are essential for maintaining moral integrity and righteousness.

Knowledge: Knowledge provides the understanding needed to navigate life's challenges and uncertainties. It offers solutions and guidance during times of trouble and is crucial for making informed decisions aligned with God's will.

Temperance: Temperance refers to self-control, especially in moments of temptation or when faced with the desire to act contrary to God's commands. It is the ability to regulate one's actions and impulses to remain aligned with spiritual principles.

Patience: Patience enables believers to wait on God's timing while continuing to grow spiritually. It encompasses the ability to endure difficulties with grace, relying on the sufficiency of God's grace to overcome challenges.

Godliness: Godliness manifests when individuals surrender their personal desires to God and live in a manner that pleases Him. It reflects a life increasingly resembling God's character and holiness.

Brotherly Kindness: This involves treating fellow believers with familial love and compassion. It signifies a relational warmth and care towards others in the Christian community, reflecting the bonds of spiritual kinship.

Charity (Agape): Agape is the highest form of love, characterized by its unconditional nature. It is not contingent on performance or personal feelings but is a deliberate choice rooted in the divine love of God. This love extends towards everyone, representing the most profound and selfless form of affection.

These concepts collectively outline the virtues essential for spiritual growth and maturity, providing a framework for believers to develop a life that mirrors the nature of God.

Chapter Ten
Step One: Faith is the foundation to living successful In the Kingdom of God

We must first grasp the critical concept of Faith — the foundational principle of the Christian life. In the Kingdom of God, everything is accessed, activated, and sustained by faith.

To enter into the Kingdom, one must take a decisive step of faith. As outlined in Romans 10:9-10, salvation is contingent upon an individual's belief and confession: "If you declare with your mouth, 'Jesus is Lord,' and believe in your heart that God raised Him from the dead, you will be saved." This passage underscores the dual process of internal belief and external confession as the means of securing salvation.

It is through faith that a person determines their eternal destiny — whether to dwell with God for eternity or to face eternal separation from Him. Faith, therefore, is not only the entry point into the Christian life but also the determining factor for one's eternal state. Thus, understanding and exercising faith is indispensable for any believer seeking to engage fully with the promises of God and the realities of His Kingdom.

Faith operates as a law, just as described in Romans 3:27: "Where then is boasting? It is excluded. By what kind of law? Of works? No, but by a law of faith." Like the law of gravity, faith functions independently of human belief or perception; it is a divine principle that governs the spiritual realm. Whether we acknowledge it or not, faith remains effective.

Faith, at its core, is acting on the Word of God. It is not rooted in human sensory experience, philosophical reasoning, or abstract theological concepts. Instead, true faith is demonstrated through alignment with God's Word. To actively engage in the operation of faith, three essential elements are required:

The Word of God: This refers both to the Logos (the written Word) and the Rhema (the spoken or revealed Word), as these provide the foundation upon which faith is built.

A Heart that Believes the Word of God: As noted in 1 Peter 3:4, faith must reside in the inner person, in the "hidden man of the heart." It requires a deep conviction that God's Word is true and reliable.

A Mouth that Speaks the Word of God: As highlighted in Proverbs 18:21, "Death and life are in the power of the tongue." Faith is activated and released through verbal confession of God's promises.

Several scriptural examples demonstrate how faith operates according to the Word of God. The most straightforward way to walk in faith is to believe God's Word so fully that it compels action. To be effective co-laborers with the Spirit of God, it is essential to understand the foundational principles of faith. Below are some biblical illustrations of the **operation of faith** as taught in Scripture:

God Spoke Creation into Existence: In the creation narrative, God demonstrates the power of spoken faith when He said, "Let there be light," and thus the world was formed. This illustrates how God's spoken word activates His creative power (**Genesis 1:3-25**).

God Changed Abram's Name to Abraham: By renaming Abram to Abraham, meaning "Father of many nations," God was calling into existence Abraham's destiny through faith, even when it was yet to be realized (**Genesis 17:3-5**).

The Conquest of Jericho: God gave specific instructions to Joshua for the conquest of Jericho, and it was through obedience to these divine commands that the walls of Jericho fell.

This example highlights how faith in action—acting on God's Word—leads to victory (**Joshua 6:1-16, 20**).

Naaman's Healing: Naaman, the Syrian general, was healed of leprosy by following the prophet Elisha's instructions to dip seven times in the Jordan River. His healing illustrates how obedience to God's Word, even when it seems illogical, brings about miraculous results (**2 Kings 5:1-4, 8-14**).

Peter Acts on the Word of God: In **Luke 5:1-9**, Peter demonstrates faith when, despite his own doubts, he obeys Jesus' instruction to cast his nets into the deep. His willingness to act on the Word of God resulted in an overwhelming catch of fish, showcasing the power of faith-filled obedience.

Each of these examples shows that faith is not merely a belief but a conviction that leads to action. Acting on the Word of God is essential for faith to manifest its transformative power.

The most straightforward approach to the operation of faith is to believe the Word of God so fully that it compels you to act upon it. One's belief is not genuine until it is expressed through action. Faith is not merely intellectual assent but is demonstrated through obedience to God's Word.

As James 1:22 admonishes, "Be doers of the Word, and not hearers only," implying that faith is incomplete without practical application.

Faith, as the Bible teaches, involves "calling those things which are not as though they were" (Romans 4:17). This principle encourages believers to speak, and act based on God's promises rather than on what is immediately visible. Instead of being governed by the natural circumstances, faith calls for the believer to declare and act according to the truth of God's Word.

In 2 Corinthians 4:13, the Apostle Paul writes, *"We have the same spirit of faith, according as it is written, I believed, and therefore I spoke; we also believe, and therefore speak."* This passage emphasizes that faith is not passive; it involves speaking in alignment with what is believed. Moreover, 2 Corinthians 4:18 reminds us that faith looks beyond the temporal and visible, stating, *"We do not look at the things which are seen, but at the things which are not seen: for the things which are seen are temporary, but the things which are not seen are eternal."*

The operation of faith calls for believers to shift their focus from the tangible, temporary realities to the unseen, eternal truths revealed in God's Word.

By doing so, believers actively participate in God's divine plan, transforming their circumstances in alignment with His eternal purposes.

The universe in which we live is governed by numerous laws, one of the most well-known being the law of gravity. This law, universally recognized, dictates that what goes up must inevitably come down. Similarly, in the spiritual realm, the principle that governs our access to the blessings and promises of God is known as the Law of Faith. This spiritual law becomes operative when we learn to "call things that be not as though they were" (Romans 4:17).

The Law of Faith functions in alignment with God's creative power, and it can only be fully engaged by those who are spiritually reborn—those who have accepted Jesus Christ as their Lord and Savior. As Romans 4:17 emphasizes, God, *"who gives life to the dead and calls into being that which does not exist,"* established this principle in His dealings with Abraham, the father of faith. God declared Abraham to be a father of many nations long before it became a physical reality, demonstrating the power of faith to bring about what is unseen.

In 2 Corinthians 4:13, Paul reinforces this truth: *"We having the same spirit of faith, according as it is written, I believed, and therefore have I spoken; we also believe, and therefore speak."* This passage underscores that faith involves not only internal belief but also the external declaration of that belief.

The Law of Faith is activated through both believing and speaking, affirming that what we confess in alignment with God's Word can bring forth His promises into our reality. Just as the law of gravity governs the physical world, the Law of Faith governs the spiritual life of believers, enabling them to operate in the supernatural and access the divine realities of God's Kingdom.

Many individuals unknowingly operate in faith from a negative perspective, often using phrases that undermine their spiritual well-being. The following examples illustrate such negative expressions and their incongruence with scriptural teachings:

1. **"My feet are killing me."** (cf. 1 Peter 2:24) – This statement contradicts the biblical promise of healing, which asserts that by Jesus' stripes, we are healed.
2. **"I am scared to death."** (cf. 2 Timothy 1:7) – This expression is contrary to the assurance that God has provided us with a spirit of power, love, and a sound mind, rather than fear.

3. **"I am broke."** (cf. Philippians 4:19) – This confession fails to acknowledge the divine promise that God will supply all our needs according to His riches in glory.
4. **"I am so weak."** (cf. Joel 3:10b) – Such a statement overlooks the scriptural directive to declare strength, as indicated by the command for the weak to proclaim, "I am strong."
5. **"I am about to lose my mind."** (cf. 1 Corinthians 2:16) – This declaration disregards the truth that believers possess the mind of Christ, which offers wisdom and stability.

These phrases reflect a negative perspective that is inconsistent with the affirmations of faith and divine promises found in Scripture. It is essential for believers to be mindful of their speech, aligning it with biblical truths to fully realize the spiritual benefits God has promised.

As believers, we possess the capacity to operate in faith even without fully comprehending its inner workings. However, it is essential to recognize that misunderstanding or misapplying faith can hinder the fulfillment of God's promises in our lives. The adversary often attempts to influence us to adopt harmful mindsets or language, as he understands that such confusion disrupts the effective application of faith.

By gaining a deeper understanding of how faith functions according to biblical principles, we position ourselves to receive the abundant blessings that God has promised.

Romans 5:1-3 offers a foundational insight into the role of faith in the believer's life: *"Therefore, being justified by faith, we have peace with God through our Lord Jesus Christ: By whom also we have access by faith into this grace wherein we stand and rejoice in hope of the glory of God. And not only so, but we glory in tribulations also: knowing that tribulation worketh patience."*

This passage highlights several key truths. First, faith justifies us before God, granting us peace with Him through Jesus Christ. Second, it is through faith that we gain access to God's grace, the enabling power by which we stand and live the Christian life. Finally, faith sustains us through trials and tribulations, producing perseverance and spiritual maturity.

As believers, we are endowed with **God's kind of faith**—a faith that not only justifies but also empowers us to access His grace and rejoice in hope, even amid difficulties. To experience the fullness of this faith, we must be diligent in acting upon it. Faith is not merely a passive belief but an active, living force that moves us to trust God's Word and apply it in every area of life.

Through the biblical examples provided, it becomes evident how the operation of faith, specifically the "God kind of faith," functions in the lives of believers. To be effective co-laborers in the work of God, it is crucial to understand the fundamental principles by which faith operates. As co-workers with the Spirit of God, we must recognize that faith is the primary means through which we access the manifold blessings God intends for us to enjoy in this life.

Moreover, it is essential to grasp that **faith is the currency of the Kingdom of God.** Everything within God's Kingdom is either accessed or activated by faith. Most significantly, faith is the means by which we are able to please God, as stated in **Hebrews 11:6:** *"But without faith it is impossible to please him: for he that cometh to God must believe that he is, and that he is a rewarder of them that diligently seek him."*

Faith not only serves as a foundational element of our relationship with God but also as the vehicle through which we interact with the divine promises and commands. To further illuminate the operations of God's faith, consider the following scriptural examples:

1. **Creation by Divine Command:** God spoke the world into existence with the words, *"Let there*

be light," establishing the creative power of faith (Genesis 1:3-25).

2. **The Name Change of Abram to Abraham:** God renamed Abram to signify his destiny as the *"Father of many nations,"* demonstrating faith in the fulfillment of His promise (Genesis 17:3-5).

3. **The Conquest of Jericho:** God gave Joshua specific instructions that led to the miraculous conquest of Jericho, exemplifying the power of obedience and faith (Joshua 6:1-16, 20).

These examples vividly illustrate that faith, when firmly anchored in the Word of God, serves as the catalyst through which divine promises are manifested and God's purposes are brought to fruition in the lives of believers. Understanding and applying the fundamental principles—or "ground rules"—of faith enables believers to actively participate in the workings of God's Kingdom, aligning themselves with the Holy Spirit to effectuate His will on earth.

One such example can be found in **2 Kings 5:1-14**, where Naaman, a Syrian army commander, experienced healing through obedience to the prophetic instruction from Elisha. His healing was not merely a result of hearing God's Word but of acting in faith, thus illustrating that divine outcomes are predicated on active faith.

Similarly, in **Luke 5:1-9**, Peter demonstrated faith in the Word of God when, despite his prior unsuccessful efforts, he obeyed Jesus' command to cast his net into the deep waters. His obedience, rooted in faith, led to a miraculous catch of fish, underscoring the importance of faith as a conduit for divine intervention.

The simplest and most effective way to operate in faith is by believing the Word of God to the point of action. True faith is not merely intellectual assent but is demonstrated through actions that align with God's promises. As **James 1:22** states, "We are not to be hearers only, but doers of the Word of God." Faith moves from belief to active participation when one steps out to demonstrate that belief through actions.

Faith, as defined in Scripture, entails "calling those things which be not as though they were" (Romans 4:17). This means that faith does not depend on sensory perceptions or external circumstances but rather on the eternal truth of God's Word.

According to **2 Corinthians 4:13**: *"We having the same spirit of faith, according as it is written, I believed, and therefore have I spoken; we also believe,* *and therefore speak."* Faith is the bold declaration of God's promises, even when the natural world seems contrary to those promises.

2 Corinthians 4:18 emphasizes this further: *"While we look not at the things which are seen, but at the things which are not seen: for the things which are seen are temporal; but the things which are not seen are eternal."*

In the universe, many natural laws govern physical phenomena—one of the most well-known being the law of gravity, which dictates that what goes up must come down. Similarly, in the spiritual realm, the law by which we access the promises and blessings of God is the **Law of Faith**. Just as gravity functions without exception, faith operates as an unwavering law within God's Kingdom, governing the believer's access to divine realities and eternal promises.

The Law of Faith operates when believers learn to "call things that be not as though they were," a principle grounded in the transformative power of faith. This law is accessible only to those who are born-again, as it is through regeneration that one gains the spiritual capacity to engage with divine realities.

In Romans 4:17, we read: "*(As it is written, I have made thee a father of many nations,) before him whom he believed, even God, who quickeneth the dead, and calleth those things which be not as though they were."*

This passage illustrates the profound nature of faith as the believer's tool to speak life into situations that, in the natural realm, appear dead or impossible. Further reinforcing this, 2 Corinthians 4:13 states: *"We having the same spirit of faith, according as it is written, I believed, and therefore have I spoken; we also believe, and therefore speak."*

Faith involves not just internal belief but also the verbal expression of that belief—articulating the promises of God over one's circumstances.

Regrettably, many individuals unwittingly operate from a negative perspective of faith, using language that undermines their spiritual well-being. Often, people make negative confessions without fully understanding their spiritual ramifications. Again, Examples include:

- **"My feet are killing me."** (cf. 1 Peter 2:24) – This statement contradicts the scriptural promise of healing, which affirms that by Jesus' stripes we are healed.
- **"I am scared to death."** (cf. 2 Timothy 1:7) – Such a confession is contrary to the biblical assurance that God has endowed us with a

spirit of power, love, and a sound mind, rather than fear.
- **"I am broke."** (cf. Philippians 4:19) – This declaration fails to acknowledge the divine promise of provision, which assures that God will meet all our needs according to His riches in glory.
- **"I am so weak."** (cf. Joel 3:10b) – This expression overlooks the scriptural exhortation to declare strength, as it commands the weak to say, "I am strong."
- **"I am about to lose my mind."** (cf. 1 Corinthians 2:16) – This statement disregards the truth that believers possess the mind of Christ, which offers wisdom and stability.

Such negative confessions can have significant spiritual implications, and it is crucial for believers to align their speech with the truths of Scripture to fully embrace and experience the spiritual benefits promised by God.

As believers, we have the ability to operate in faith, even when we lack a full understanding of its dynamics. The enemy exploits this ignorance by influencing us to make negative declarations that hinder our spiritual growth and blessings. By learning and understanding the proper workings of faith, we can align ourselves with God's promises and receive the abundant blessings He intends for us. The power of life and death lies in the tongue, and believers must consciously choose to speak life, as Scripture instructs.

According to Romans 5:1-3, Scripture affirms: *"Therefore being justified by faith, we have peace with God through our Lord Jesus Christ; by whom also we have access by faith into this grace wherein we stand and rejoice in hope of the glory of God. And not only so, but we glory in tribulations also: knowing that tribulation worketh patience."*

This passage underscores the foundational role of faith in the Christian life, as it is through faith that we are justified and enter into peace with God. Furthermore, faith grants us access to divine grace, which enables us to stand firm and rejoice, even in the midst of trials, knowing that such tribulations cultivate spiritual endurance and patience. As believers, we are endowed with the "God-kind of faith," a dynamic force that not only justifies but also empowers us to partake in the divine nature.

To be effective co-laborers with the Spirit of God, it is essential to understand the fundamental principles that govern the operation of this faith. Only by aligning ourselves with these "ground rules" can we collaborate with the Spirit in fulfilling God's purposes on earth. Faith is the spiritual currency of the Kingdom of God, through which all heavenly resources are accessed and activated. Every blessing, promise, and provision of God is unlocked by faith, making it the primary means by which we engage with God's Kingdom. Most importantly, as stated in Hebrews 11:6, *"But without faith it is impossible to please him: for he that cometh to God must believe that he is, and that he is a rewarder of them that diligently seek him."*

This verse highlights that faith is indispensable for pleasing God, for it not only affirms His existence but also acknowledges His generous nature toward those who earnestly seek Him.

Faith is not merely a theological concept but the active principle by which we engage with and experience the fullness of God's blessings in this life. The believer's journey of faith is one of continual trust, obedience, and cooperation with God's Spirit, leading to a life that reflects His glory and purpose.

Chapter Eleven
Step Two: Virtue is the moral compass for Kingdom living.

In the context of God's maturity plan, the second step is virtue.

I. What is Virtue?

Virtue is a concept frequently delineated as moral excellence, encompassing attributes such as goodness and righteousness. According to the Webster Dictionary, virtue refers to the "conformity of one's life and conduct to moral and ethical principles and uprightness."

In moral and scholarly discourse, virtues are understood as enduring attitudes, dispositions, or character traits that enable individuals to embody and enact moral behaviors. These virtues such as honesty, courage, compassion, generosity, fidelity, integrity, fairness, self-control, and prudence serve as foundational elements of ethical conduct. Virtues are also characterized as habits, signifying that, once cultivated, they become intrinsic to an individual's character. For instance, a person who has internalized the virtue of generosity is consistently described as generous, given that they exhibit this trait in various contexts and interactions.

This habitual manifestation underscores the role of virtue in shaping moral identity and behavior.

Jesus as the Embodiment of Virtue

In Christian theology, Jesus Christ is perceived as the epitome of virtue, serving as the quintessential exemplar for believers. The directive to emulate Christ entails aspiring to become "little Christs," striving to replicate His actions and character. This transformative process is aimed at achieving moral and spiritual perfection, reflecting the divine ideal. Following Christ's paradigm, the virtues to be adopted by believers include charity, courage, faith, humility, justice, knowledge, wisdom, obedience, perseverance, faithfulness, prudence, and temperance. These virtues are integral to Christian moral philosophy, symbolizing the manifestation of divine attributes within individuals.

Christian moral virtues are understood as a reflection of God's nature within human beings. The call to embody virtues such as godly excellence, goodness, and righteousness is seen as a divine mandate. Furthermore, Christian virtues are aligned with the pursuit of attributes that are true, honest, just, pure, lovely, and commendable, thereby embodying the ethical and moral ideals prescribed by Christian teachings.

Philippians 4:8-9 and the Pursuit of Virtue

Philippians 4:8-9 presents a directive for moral and ethical contemplation:

> *"Finally, brethren, whatsoever things are true, whatsoever things are honest, whatsoever things are just, whatsoever things are pure, whatsoever things are lovely, whatsoever things are of good report; if there be any virtue, and if there be any praise, think on these things. 9 Those things, which ye have both learned, and received, and heard, and seen in me, do: and the God of peace shall be with you."*

This passage underscores the importance of focusing on virtues and moral excellence as foundational elements of a Christian life. It instructs believers to engage in reflective thought upon things that are true, honest, just, pure, lovely, and commendable. The promise of divine peace accompanies adherence to these virtues and practices.

God's calling is manifest through Jesus Christ. Accepting Jesus Christ as Lord and Savior is believed to invoke God's provision of all necessary resources for both earthly and spiritual well-being. God's divine power is considered sufficient to equip believers with everything necessary for life and godliness.

This relationship with God facilitates participation in His glory and virtue.

In examining personal development, one might consider what constitutes a person of virtue, moral integrity, and character. Essential questions arise: What kind of person do I aspire to become? Which virtues align with this ideal self? What actions will foster the virtues I aim to develop? What behaviors will reflect the character I seek to embody? Engaging with these questions can guide the cultivation of a virtuous and morally sound life.

Development of Moral Virtues

The cultivation of moral virtues involves a process of both learning and practical application. As the ancient philosopher Aristotle posited, character development is achieved through disciplined practice, while repeated self-indulgence can lead to moral corruption. Just as physical endurance is honed through rigorous training, so too is moral character refined through habitual engagement with virtues such as fairness, courage, and compassion.

In Philippians 4:8, the virtues of God are revealed through the teachings of Jesus Christ.

These Christian virtues include truth, honesty, righteousness, purity, love, and goodness. The pursuit of these virtues is facilitated by self-control, which can be developed through meditation on the virtues exemplified by Christ. According to Christian doctrine, Jesus empowers believers to embody divine virtues and overcome the enticements of sin.

2 Peter 1:3 reinforces the divine call to embrace Christian virtues, asserting that God's divine power provides believers with all necessary resources for life and godliness. The verse states: *"According as his divine power hath given unto us all things that pertain unto life and godliness, through the knowledge of him that hath called us to glory and virtue."*

In the Christian tradition, the indwelling of the Holy Spirit serves as a source of inspiration for virtue. Many Christians interpret their conscience as the 'voice of God,' guiding their moral decisions.

Furthermore, the practice of active prayer, whether for guidance or intervention, is integral to Christian living. This responsive and God-centered approach engages the whole person in the pursuit of faith, hope, and love, maintaining focus on the divine source of all true virtue.

The Acquisition of Virtue According to Scripture

In 2 Peter 1:3, it is stated that "God's divine power has given us everything we need for life and godliness through our knowledge of him who called us by his own glory and goodness." This passage underscores that the potential for a virtuous life is provided by divine provision, though its actualization depends on human choice. Virtue, in Christian understanding, is fundamentally rooted in charity and humility, which stand in contrast to selfishness and pride.

The practice of virtue is perceived as an expression of love; thus, genuine love inherently involves virtuous conduct. The interconnectedness of love and virtue implies that one cannot truly love without embodying virtue. Furthermore, *1 Corinthians 1:22-25 elucidates the nature of divine provision in relation to human effort: "For the Jews require a sign, and the Greeks seek after wisdom:* [23] *But we preach Christ crucified, unto the Jews a stumbling block, and unto the Greeks foolishness;* [24] *But unto them which are called, both Jews and Greeks, Christ the power of God, and the wisdom of God.* [25] *Because the foolishness of God is wiser than men; and the weakness of God is stronger than men."*

This passage emphasizes that the gospel reveals that God's grace, as embodied in the crucifixion of Christ, provides what human reason and moral effort alone cannot achieve. Virtues are not merely the result of self-generated effort but are seen as gifts from God. However, these gifts necessitate human cooperation and active engagement, illustrating that while virtues are divinely bestowed, their manifestation requires human volition and effort.

The Formation of Negative Moral Traits

The New Testament instructs believers to focus on virtuous thoughts and behaviors as indicated in Philippians 4:8. Christian virtues encompass qualities such as truth, honesty, righteousness, purity, love, and goodness. In contrast, negative moral traits or evil virtues are antithetical to these Christian principles and should ideally be absent from the Christian life.

The concept of moral deterioration or the development of evil virtues can be understood through the inverse of Christian virtues. Therefore, traits such as deceit, dishonesty, injustice, impurity, hatred, and malevolence represent the perversion of the virtues prescribed by Christian ethics and should be avoided.

Step Two: Virtue is the moral compass for Kingdom living.   119

An illustrative historical example is found in Leviticus, which describes the Israelites' 400-year sojourn in Egypt. During this period, the Israelites were exposed to cultural and moral influences that were contrary to the divine standards of conduct. This extended exposure to a morally divergent environment contributed to the formation of traits and behaviors inconsistent with God's laws and virtues.

This book offers guidelines for virtuous living when living in a time or place that does not honor God's ways. These guidelines include: (Book of Leviticus) Sexual sins are like a downward sparrow! Only hell knows what next because that's where people are headed that does such things. (Leviticus 20:1-27).

Sexual sins are like a downward sparrow! Only hell knows what next because that's where people are headed that does such things.

Guidelines for the different Offerings Chapters 1-6.
Guidelines for the Law of the Offerings 7-7
Guidelines for the Consecration Chapters 8-9
Examples for break the rules "God laws" Cpts 10-20
Gods cleansing procedures Chapters 11-17
Gods Atonements Chapters 16-17
The Relationship of God's people Chapters 18-22
The Feasts of Jehovah Chapters 23
Instructions - Warnings Chapters 24-27 Vs 20:1-27.

"And the LORD Spake unto Moses, saying, ² Again, thou shalt say to the children of Israel, Whosoever he be of the children of Israel, or of the strangers that sojourn in Israel, that giveth any of his seed unto Molech; he shall surely be put to death: the people of the land shall stone him with stones. ³ And I will set my face against that man and will cut him off from among his people; because he hath given of his seed unto Molech, to defile my sanctuary, and to profane my holy name. ⁴ And if the people of the land do any ways hide their eyes from the man, when he giveth of his seed unto Molech, and kill him not: ⁵ Then I will set my face against that man, and against his family, and will cut him off, and all that go a whoring after him, to commit whoredom with Molech, from among their people. ⁶And the soul that turneth after such as have familiar spirits, and after wizards, to go a whoring after them, I will even set my face against that soul and will cut him off from among his people. ⁷ Sanctify yourselves therefore and be ye holy: for I am the LORD your God. ⁸ And ye shall keep my statutes and do them: I am the LORD which sanctify you. ⁹ For everyone that curseth his father or his mother shall be surely put to death: he hath cursed his father or his mother; his blood shall be upon him.

Sin of adultery

10 And the man that committeth adultery with another man's wife, even he that committeth adultery with his neighbour's wife, the adulterer and the adulteress shall surely be put to death. 11 And the man that lieth with his father's wife hath uncovered his father's nakedness: both of them shall surely be put to death; their blood shall be upon them. 12 And if a man lie with his daughter in law, both of them shall surely be put to death: they have wrought confusion; their blood shall be upon them. 13 If a man also lies with mankind, as he lieth with a woman, both of them have committed an abomination: they shall surely be put to death; their blood shall be upon them. 14 And if a man takes a wife and her mother, it is wickedness: they shall be burnt with fire, both he and they; that there be no wickedness among you. 15 And if a man lie with a beast, he shall surely be put to death: and ye shall slay the beast. 16 And if a woman approach unto any beast, and lie down thereto, thou shalt kill the woman, and the beast: they shall surely be put to death; their blood shall be upon them. 17 And if a man shall take his sister, his father's daughter, or his mother's daughter, and see her nakedness, and she see his nakedness; it is a wicked thing; and they shall be cut off in the sight of their people: he hath uncovered his sister's nakedness; he shall bear his iniquity.

18 And if a man shall lie with a woman having her sickness and shall uncover her nakedness; he hath discovered her fountain, and she hath uncovered the fountain of her blood: and both of them shall be cut off from among their people. [19] *And thou shalt not uncover the nakedness of thy mother's sister, nor of thy father's sister: for he uncovereth his near kin: they shall bear their iniquity.* [20] *And if a man shall lie with his uncle's wife, he hath uncovered his uncle's nakedness: they shall bear their sin; they shall die childless.* [21] *And if a man shall take his brother's wife, it is an unclean thing: he hath uncovered his brother's nakedness; they shall be childless.*

Obedience is required with holiness

[22] *Ye shall therefore keep all my statutes, and all my therein, spue you not out.* [23] *And ye shall not walk in the manners of the nation, which I cast out before you: for they committed all these things, and therefore I abhorred them.* [24] *But I have said unto you, Ye shall inherit their land, and I will give it unto you to possess it, a land that floweth with milk and honey: I am the LORD your God, which have separated you from other people.* [25] *Ye shall therefore put difference between clean beasts and unclean, and between unclean fowls and clean: and ye shall not make your souls abominable by beast, or by fowl, or by any manner of living thing that creepeth on the ground, which I have separated from you as unclean.* [26] *And ye shall be holy unto me: for I the LORD am holy, and have severed you from other people, that ye should be mine.* [27] *A man also or woman that hath a familiar spirit, or that is a wizard, shall surely be put to death: they shall stone them with stones: their blood shall be upon them.*

We gain bad morals and virtues:

By what you watch; what you read; what or who you hang around with will influence you; and what you hear. Some examples of bad virtues Include: stealing, lying, sex contrary to God's Word, pornography, lust, drinking, drugs, bad language and rebellion. These are all shaped by a life outside of God's virtues. What are the benefits of good virtue? It is just like a good name there is no price that you can put on a good name.

According to Proverbs 22:1; *"A good name is to be chosen rather than great riches, Loving favor rather than silver and gold."* As a child of God, we carry the name of Christ on our shoulders. " If a Christian's desire is to mature, it is crucial that they have virtue of character.

Chapter Twelve
Step Three: The Knowledge of God

The third stage in spiritual maturation is the acquisition of knowledge, which must be integrated into our spiritual nourishment. This prompts a critical inquiry: Why is it imperative for Christians to engage in a comprehensive reading of the Bible?

1. Knowledge of God

The concept of divine omniscience is central to understanding the necessity of thorough biblical study. According to theological doctrine, God possesses perfect knowledge of all things—both conceivable and actual. This includes comprehensive awareness of past, present, and future events, as well as the intricacies of every individual's existence across the realms of heaven, earth, and hell.

As delineated in Daniel 2:22, "He knoweth what is in the darkness," indicating that nothing eludes His perception; nothing remains concealed from Him, and nothing is forgotten, save for our sins. This notion underscores the profundity of divine awareness and the extent of God's omniscient insight.

Isaiah 43:25 further elucidates this by stating, "I, even I, am he that blotteth out thy transgressions for mine own sake and will not remember thy sins." Here, the text emphasizes that while God is all-knowing, He intentionally chooses to forget our transgressions as an act of divine grace.

The infinite scope of God's knowledge should inspire profound reverence. The Lord's wisdom far surpasses that of the most learned human being. Whereas humans are often uncertain about what the future holds, God's omniscient perspective encompasses all possible outcomes and events, affirming His supreme understanding and authority.

The boundless scope of God's omniscience should elicit a profound sense of reverence and awe. The divine awareness encompasses all aspects of human activity—every action, utterance, and thought are within His purview. Proverbs 15:3 asserts, "The eyes of the Lord are in every place, beholding the evil and the good," underscoring the comprehensive nature of God's surveillance.

This realization carries significant implications for the believer. A deeper engagement with the Word of God could profoundly influence behavior, fostering a mindset that aligns with divine observance.

In reflecting upon this truth, one might adopt the posture of Hagar, who, in Genesis 16:13, acknowledged, "Thou God, seest me." This recognition of God's omniscient presence should inspire a heightened sense of reverence and adoration within the Christian heart. From the inception of my existence, our entire life has been visible to God. He foresaw every instance of my failings, sins, and periods of spiritual regression; nevertheless, He remained steadfast in His commitment to me. This profound awareness of divine omniscience should inspire deep humility and reverence in our worship.

The pursuit of personal knowledge serves a dual purpose: it equips me with the insights needed to navigate life's challenges and uncertainties, thereby fortifying me against the manipulative strategies of the adversary. In other words, acquiring knowledge aims to render me less vulnerable to spiritual deception.

Humanity was created in the image of God with the ultimate objective of living for His glory. Although this divine image is marred by sin, it still provides a genuine, though not exhaustive, understanding of God. Those who experience regeneration through the new birth and engage with the Scriptures are positioned to fulfill the purpose of living for God's glory.

Romans 15:14 encapsulates this aspiration: "filled with all knowledge."

2. Knowledge as Distinct from Information and Education

Knowledge, when divorced from its divine origin, is rendered ineffectual. In the absence of God, knowledge lacks purpose and merely fosters arrogance, as indicated by 1 Corinthians 8:1: "Knowledge puffs up, but love builds up." This underscores that while knowledge alone can be detrimental and lead to pride, it is God's guidance that imbues knowledge with its true value and directs it towards fulfilling our ultimate purpose.

Divine knowledge transcends mere information and education. It constitutes a profound confidence and calm assurance in the veracity of what is known, regardless of personal feelings or external influences. This form of knowledge entails an intimate and comprehensive understanding — an in-depth acquaintance with truths rather than a superficial engagement. For instance, knowing God involves a deep relationship with Him, seeking not just to understand Him but to experience Him more fully, as articulated in 2 Timothy 1:12 and Philippians 3:10.

Similarly, our engagement with the Bible should aim for a profound grasp of its teachings. While initial knowledge of biblical truths is important, the goal is to explore the rich depths of its wisdom, as expressed in Romans 11:33, which speaks to the "depths of the riches" found in divine knowledge.

In relational contexts, such as understanding a spouse as described in 1 Peter 3:7, true knowledge involves continuous learning and improvement, paralleling how one enhances professional skills to achieve advancement and success. This principle of ongoing growth and deeper comprehension applies universally, reflecting the need for persistent effort and dedication to gain a fuller understanding and improve our interactions and performance.

Knowledge must be substantiated by evidence; it requires validation beyond mere conjecture or subjective feeling. In the realm of Christian growth, knowledge is not static but an evolving pursuit, as articulated in 2 Peter 3:18, which urges believers to "grow in the grace and knowledge of our Lord and Savior Jesus Christ." It is imperative that Christians continually expand their understanding of divine truths and avoid complacency.

Initial conversion to Christ involves acquiring fundamental knowledge, akin to learning the basic elements of faith. However, this foundational understanding is only the beginning—much like learning the ABCs before mastering the entire alphabet. The process of spiritual maturation involves progressing from elementary doctrines to more complex theological insights.

The metaphor of spiritual nourishment reflects this growth: one begins with "milk," digesting simple truths, and gradually advances to "solid food," which includes more profound and substantial teachings. This progression is complemented by the addition of "salt" for flavor and "honey" for encouragement, illustrating the importance of both robust instruction and uplifting reinforcement.

As emphasized in 2 Peter 1:5, believers are encouraged to consistently engage with the Scriptures whether through reading, meditation, or reflection. Even during periods of rest, the mind should remain attuned to divine teachings, applying the truths of Scripture to daily life. Philippians 4:8 supports this practice, advocating for a mindset that continually reflects on the virtues and truths of God's Word, ensuring that spiritual growth is both intentional and integrative.

A comprehensive and profound understanding of theological concepts is essential for spiritual growth. This necessity is underscored in

2 Peter 3:15-16, which states:
> *"And account that the longsuffering of our Lord is salvation; even as our beloved brother Paul also according to the wisdom given unto him hath written unto you; as also in all his epistles, speaking in them of these things; in which are some things hard to be understood, which they that are unlearned and unstable wrest, as they do also the other scriptures, unto their own destruction."*

This passage highlights that certain elements of Scripture, including those found in Paul's writings, can be challenging to comprehend. Those who lack sufficient knowledge and stability may distort these difficult teachings, leading to their own ruin. Therefore, it is crucial not merely to acknowledge the presence of these teachings but to thoroughly understand, experience, and embody them. Ignorance does not foster spiritual maturity, nor does it contribute to the growth of a Christian. John 8:31-32 further emphasizes the importance of truth in achieving freedom:
> *"Then said Jesus to those Jews which believed on him, If ye continue in my word, then are ye*

> *my disciples indeed; and ye shall know the truth, and the truth shall make you free."*

Here, Jesus asserts that true discipleship involves persistent engagement with His teachings, which leads to an understanding of the truth that liberates. The Bereans, as described in Acts 17:11, exemplify this approach by diligently examining the Scriptures:

> *"Now these were more noble than those in Thessalonica, in that they received the word with all readiness of mind, and searched the scriptures daily, whether those things were so."*

Their commitment to scrutinizing the Scriptures underscores the importance of rigorous and proactive study in the pursuit of spiritual truth and maturity.

The Bereans are described as having exhibited greater nobility than the Thessalonians due to their diligent approach to receiving and examining the word of God. Acts 17:11 states:

> *"These were more noble than those in Thessalonica, in that they received the word with all readiness of mind, and searched the scriptures daily, whether those things were so."*

This passage highlights the Bereans commendable practice of accepting new teachings with an open mind and rigorously verifying their accuracy through daily Scripture examination.

In the process of engaging with the Bible, one must approach it with a methodical and thoughtful strategy. Some biblical concepts are akin to solid food that requires thorough chewing before it can be properly assimilated. This analogy emphasizes the necessity of in-depth study rather than superficial reading. To effectively interpret Scripture, the following steps are recommended:

1. **Read the Context**: Understand the broader narrative and historical setting of the passage to grasp its full meaning.
2. **Ask the Questions**: Pose critical questions about the text to clarify its implications and relevance.
3. **Look Up Cross-References**: Utilize cross-references, often provided in study Bibles, to connect related passages and gain a more comprehensive understanding.

Determining the validity of a teaching or belief requires comparison with the revealed truth of God's Word. The key to being accepted by Jehovah is a deep understanding and adherence to this divine truth.

Consequently, a maturing Christian should prioritize regular attendance at all gatherings of the faith community — whether for worship, study, or fellowship.

Such commitment reflects a seriousness about spiritual growth and an unwillingness to let trivial matters interfere with participation in these essential activities.

Certain concepts must be experienced to be fully comprehended. For instance, the principles of tithing, offerings, and the gifts of love, as well as the practice of sowing and reaping, cannot be fully understood through theoretical knowledge alone. One must engage in the act of giving to appreciate the associated blessings. Similarly, the virtues of patience and endurance are best grasped through personal trials and challenges, which illuminate the value of grace and perseverance.

3. The Necessity of Growing in Biblical Knowledge

A Christian's life devoid of ongoing growth in Biblical knowledge is analogous to that of a "dead man or woman walking" — dry, empty, and devoid of spiritual vitality. Mere accumulation of information — facts, figures, and names — without deeper understanding remains superficial.

True knowledge involves grasping the underlying principles, moral teachings, and the "why" behind biblical events and doctrines.

Such knowledge transcends rote memorization and enriches the believer's spiritual journey, akin to a vibrant, dynamic relationship rather than a static one. Marriage, as an illustration, should remain intriguing and continually explored, reflecting the evolving nature of understanding and engagement, as advised in 1 Peter 3:7:

> *"Likewise, ye husbands, dwell with them according to knowledge, giving honour unto the wife, as unto the weaker vessel, and as being heirs together of the grace of life; that your prayers be not hindered."*

This passage underscores the importance of ongoing growth and discovery within relationships, paralleling the need for continual development and deeper understanding in one's spiritual life.

Likewise, ye husbands, dwell with *them* according to knowledge, giving honour unto the wife, as unto the weaker vessel, and as being heirs together of the grace of life; that your prayers be not hindered.

Engaging with the Bible should be approached with the enthusiasm and curiosity of a treasure hunt. This metaphor emphasizes the profound value and discovery inherent in Scripture, akin to seeking out hidden treasures. Additionally, prayer should be regarded as a means to access abundant grace, as highlighted in James 5:16:

"Confess your faults one to another, and pray one for another, that ye may be healed. The effectual fervent prayer of a righteous man availeth much."

4. How to Grow in Knowledge of God

To deepen one's knowledge of God, it is essential to systematically explore Scripture and actively engage in learning. Utilizing a notebook to record insights and questions can facilitate this process. Regular attendance at church services, participation in discipleship lessons, and enrollment in a Bible Institute are practical ways to enhance understanding.

A valuable measure of one's knowledge is the ability to teach others. In preparing to answer questions and explain concepts, you will likely experience personal growth. The aim of discipleship is to acquire and apply knowledge meaningfully. A contemporary issue in ministry is that some ministers and pastors teach from second-hand information rather than firsthand understanding, potentially diminishing the effectiveness of their teaching.

A willingness to adjust one's perspective when confronted with new, biblically-aligned truths is crucial.
Ensure that your knowledge remains practical and is harmonized with love, as advised in Hebrews 13:9:
> *"Be not carried about with divers and strange doctrines. For it is a good thing that the heart be established with grace; not with meats, which have not profited them that have been occupied therein."*

This passage underscores the importance of grounding one's heart in grace rather than being swayed by diverse or novel teachings. Balancing knowledge with love and practical application is key to spiritual growth.

1 Corinthians 8:1-2.
> *"Now as touching things offered unto idols, we know that we all have knowledge. Knowledge puffeth up, but charity edifieth."*

If we are to be diligent and steadfast Christians, equipped to stand firm against the schemes of the adversary, nothing is more essential than an earnest and disciplined study of the Word of God.

The vast expanse of available literature — though often valuable and enriching — pales in comparison to the singular importance of the Scriptures. The sheer volume of written works, even those classified as beneficial or spiritually edifying, far exceeds the capacity of any one individual to engage with in a single lifetime. Yet, amidst this overwhelming sea of knowledge, there is one book that demands our utmost attention and commitment: the Bible. It is not simply a matter of preference, but a divine imperative that we invest our time and energy in its study, lest we remain spiritually ignorant and ill-equipped for the challenges of faith. To neglect the Word of God is to jeopardize our spiritual vitality, for it alone provides the wisdom, truth, and authority necessary for both personal transformation and effective resistance against the forces of darkness.

The Holy Bible must be read comprehensively, from Genesis to Revelation, repeatedly and with deliberate engagement. This is not to achieve a mere cursory familiarity, as one might casually browse a newspaper, selectively absorbing fragments of information. Rather, we must immerse ourselves in its entirety, becoming intimately acquainted with its language, internalizing its ready application to life. The very tone, spirit, and essence of Scripture must shape our thinking and character.

The Word of God, the Bible, stands as the ultimate and authoritative standard of truth. Human faculties of sense and reason, divinely created, exist for the purpose of receiving and processing God's revelation.

In doing so, humanity is called to align its thoughts with God's, thinking His thoughts after Him. Human beings were created to interpret knowledge through the lens of dependence on divine revelation. Therefore, all things in the universe must be understood and interpreted in relation to God, His purposes, and His sovereign plan for creation.

Chapter Thirteen

Step Four: "Add to knowledge Temperance" (Self-control)

The fourth crucial step in the journey toward spiritual maturity is temperance. Temperance, or self-control, enables individuals to govern their desires and impulses, particularly when faced with the temptation to do wrong. The concept of balance is central to the biblical understanding of this virtue. In the second epistle of Peter, specifically in chapter 1, the apostle emphasizes the importance of progressive spiritual growth, instructing believers to build upon their foundation of salvation. He exhorts them to "add to your virtue knowledge, and to knowledge temperance" (2 Peter 1:5-6.)

The term "temperance," however, is frequently misinterpreted. Far from merely implying moderation in external behaviors, it encompasses a deeper spiritual discipline: the ability to exercise restraint and mastery over one's internal desires, particularly in relation to moral and ethical decision-making. This self-governance is essential for sustaining a life that reflects Christ-like character, marking a critical milestone in the believer's path to spiritual maturity.

Are you a balanced person?

When reflecting on the concept of balance, I envision an individual who exercises comprehensive control over various aspects of life. Such a person effectively manages their relationships with God, spouse, children, and community, demonstrating an ability to allocate appropriate time and energy to each. They maintain a healthy equilibrium between work, home, and recreational activities, ensuring that no single area of their life dominates at the expense of others. This balance reflects a well-ordered life where priorities are carefully calibrated and harmonized.

In many modern translations, the term "temperance" is often rendered as "self-control." While self-control is indeed a significant component of temperance, I contend that the term encompasses a broader and deeper meaning. Some may associate the word "temperance" with the historical Temperance Movement, which advocated for abstinence from alcohol, and thus may assume it primarily refers to refraining from drinking. While there may be value in that interpretation, it does not capture the full essence of what temperance truly signifies in a biblical context.

Temperance, as used in Scripture, refers to a comprehensive discipline of the self—a measured and thoughtful restraint that governs not just physical appetites, but all dimensions of human behavior, thought, and action, in alignment with God's will.

Step Four: "Add to knowledge Temperance" (Self-control)

According to 1 Corinthians 9:25, *"And every man that striveth for the mastery is temperate in all things. Now they do it to obtain a corruptible crown; but we an incorruptible."*

Scripture instructs that individuals who seek to live in accordance with God's will we must strive to practice temperance in all aspects of life. The root of the term "temperance" derives from "temper," which, contrary to common misconceptions, is not inherently negative. When we hear someone say, "I have a temper," we often associate it with uncontrolled anger or impulsivity. However, the issue arises not from having a temper, but from losing control of it. Temper, in its proper and balanced form, is a natural and necessary part of human disposition. The goal for godly individuals is to cultivate a temperament that is measured, moderate, and even-keeled.

This reflects the broader biblical principle of temperance—exercising self-regulation and maintaining balance in one's emotional, mental, and behavioral responses in alignment with spiritual maturity.

Jesus provides a profound example of temper—specifically, anger under control—in the account found in John 2:13-15. In this passage, Jesus enters the temple in Jerusalem and, upon witnessing the desecration of the sacred space by merchants and money changers, responds with righteous indignation.

He fashions a whip out of cords and drives them out, overturning their tables and exclaiming that they had turned His Father's house into a marketplace.

This incident illustrates that Jesus' display of anger was not an uncontrolled or impulsive outburst but a measured and purposeful response to the violation of divine sanctity. His actions were governed by a profound sense of justice and zeal for the holiness of God's house, reflecting the biblical ideal of temperance — anger exercised under control, in service of righteousness rather than personal frustration. Through this, Jesus models the proper use of temper, demonstrating that even strong emotions, when channeled in alignment with God's will, serve a constructive and redemptive purpose. John 2:13-15, *"[13]And the Jews' Passover was at hand and Jesus went up to Jerusalem; [14]And found in the temple those that sold oxen and sheep and doves, and the changers of money sitting: [15]And when he had made a scourge of small cords, he drove them all out of the temple, and the sheep, and the oxen; and poured out the changers' money, and overthrew the tables;"*

Temperance does not imply complacency in one's faith. It is not a call to be passive or indifferent toward spiritual matters. On the contrary, believers are exhorted to pursue God with zeal and passion, continually striving to lead others to Him.

This pursuit, however, must be tempered by an attitude of love, kindness, and gentleness. Evangelism should never be marked by harshness or insensitivity; rather, it should reflect Christ's grace and compassion.

At its core, temperance refers to the ongoing practice of moderation and self-restraint. It is an essential Christian virtue because it stands in direct opposition to the sinful nature, which even believers must contend with. The sin nature seeks to gratify the desires of the flesh, often manifesting in impulsive or self-indulgent behaviors. Temperance, therefore, is a safeguard against these inclinations, enabling Christians to exercise self-control and remain disciplined in their walk with God.

To achieve victory in the Christian life, self-control is indispensable. It enables the believer to persist in spiritual disciplines while resisting behaviors and actions that appeal to fleshly desires. Importantly, temperance is not an attribute that develops instantaneously; it is cultivated over time through intentional and conscious effort. It is a virtue that requires ongoing diligence and practice, contributing to a well-rounded, mature Christian character.

In the professional environment, temperance can be likened to adhering to organizational standards, resisting the temptation to cut corners, and maintaining a consistent, steady, and dependable work ethic.

This quality is highly valued in the workplace and is often regarded as a key indicator of success. It reflects an individual's capacity for self-regulation and long-term reliability, both of which are essential for sustainable achievement.

Proverbs 25:28 offers a vivid illustration of the consequences of lacking self-control: "He that hath no rule over his own spirit is like a city that is broken down, and without walls." This imagery conveys the vulnerability and disorder that arise when an individual fails to exercise discipline and restraint. Similarly, Romans 6:16-18 highlights the critical choice between submission to sin or obedience to righteousness. Those who fail to govern their impulses become slaves to sin, leading to spiritual death. However, through obedience to the principles of righteousness, believers are liberated from sin and empowered to live in accordance with God's will.

The scriptures collectively underscore that temperance is not merely self-control, but the strength to apply knowledge in practical ways. Proverbs 16:32 further emphasizes the value of temperance, declaring that "He that is slow to anger is better than the mighty, and he that ruleth his spirit than he that taketh a city." This verse places the virtue of temperance above even physical strength or military conquest, illustrating its profound significance in the life of the believer.

James 1:19-20 encourages believers to be "swift to hear, slow to speak, slow to wrath," recognizing that human anger does not accomplish the righteousness of God. Galatians 5:22-23 lists temperance among the fruits of the Spirit, affirming that it is a divinely inspired attribute that cannot be overruled by any human law. Likewise, Titus 2:2 calls for mature men to be "sober, grave, temperate, sound in faith, in charity, in patience," further demonstrating that temperance is integral to Christian maturity and the formation of godly character.

In conclusion, temperance represents the capacity to transform knowledge into disciplined action, exercising control over one's impulses in accordance with God's will.

This virtue is indispensable not only for personal spiritual development but also for professional integrity and success. Without self-control, individuals may become susceptible to the influence and manipulation of satanic forces. To safeguard against spiritual decline, believers are called to build upon their faith by adding virtue, to virtue knowledge, and to knowledge temperance, as outlined in 2 Peter 1:5-6.

The sequential nature of these virtues is critical, as each builds upon the other, forming a cohesive foundation for spiritual resilience. If any of these elements are neglected, the promise of spiritual steadfastness becomes uncertain. As the Apostle Peter warns, there is no assurance of remaining steadfast if these virtues are abandoned. However, he offers a profound guarantee for those who diligently cultivate them: "You will never fall" (2 Peter 1:10). This progression underscores the interconnectedness of faith, virtue, knowledge, and temperance, which together serve as the pillars of a life that remains firmly rooted in Christ.

Chapter Fourteen
Step Five: "Add to Temperance" (Patience)

Faith serves as the entry point into the family of God and establishes the foundational structure for our entire Christian journey. It is through faith that we gain access to divine grace and begin our spiritual formation. Virtue, then, acts as a safeguard, protecting us from being ensnared by sin and preventing spiritual defeat. Knowledge equips us with the necessary insights to navigate life's challenges, providing clarity in moments of uncertainty and turmoil. In essence, when we possess the right knowledge, we are less vulnerable to the devil's distractions, for understanding undermines his ability to deceive.

Temperance, or self-control, empowers us to restrain ourselves when tempted to do wrong, further fortifying our spiritual walk. It builds upon faith, virtue, and knowledge, ensuring that our actions remain aligned with God's will.

The fifth stage of spiritual maturity is patience. Patience is not merely passive waiting but embodies endurance—marked by staying power, stamina, and fortitude. It is the ability to persist in the face of frustration, adversity, or pain without succumbing to complaint, irritation, or anger. Patience, therefore, reflects a deep-rooted spiritual strength, enabling believers to persevere through life's trials while maintaining an unwavering trust in God's providence and timing.

The necessity of patience in the Christian life arises from several key factors. Firstly, our flesh remains imperfect and resistant to immediate change, often failing to align with God's expectations swiftly. Secondly, our souls may struggle to assimilate wisdom at the pace desired, impeding our spiritual growth. Additionally, the timing of answered prayers frequently does not coincide with our own expectations, necessitating patience in our trust and waiting.

Patience is crucial for navigating trials and difficulties, providing direction and resilience in the face of adversity. A profound understanding of patience enables us to draw strength from our waiting period, as articulated in Isaiah 40:31: "But they that wait upon the LORD shall renew their strength; they shall mount up with wings as eagles; they shall run, and not be weary; and they shall walk, and not faint." This verse highlights the transformative power of patience, suggesting that enduring faith in God will result in renewed vigor and perseverance.

Moreover, Proverbs 13:12 elucidates the emotional impact of deferred hope: "Hope deferred maketh the heart sick: but when the desire cometh, it is a tree of life."

Step Five: "Add to Temperance" (Patience)

The Contemporary English Version (CEV) offers a more vivid interpretation: "Not getting what you want can make you feel sick, but a wish that comes true is a life-giving tree." This proverb underscores the significant psychological and spiritual effect of patience and the eventual fulfillment of our desires, which revitalizes and sustains us. Patience, therefore, is not merely a passive waiting but an active engagement with God's timing, crucial for maintaining spiritual well-being and resilience.

I made mention that you are never to pray for patience, because it a hard word to live, in simple words it means waiting, and not getting upset while you wait. Patience is the opposites of haste, stress out, worry, and anxiety.

As children of God, we are called to live free from anxiety, as indicated by Philippians 4:6: "Don't worry about anything, but pray about everything, with thankful hearts offer up your prayers and requests to God" (CEV). This passage underscores the importance of replacing worry with prayer, framed by a spirit of gratitude.

Impatience manifests in several ways, including:

1. **Irritability**, Stress, and Frustration: Patience stands in opposition to these negative emotional states. It is a virtue that resists being swayed by external circumstances, contrasting sharply with

despondency. Patience is inherently linked to faith, as it reflects a steadfast trust in God's timing and promises.

2. **The Challenges of Patience**: Patience is not an innate quality but one that must be cultivated through experiences of adversity. It is developed through trials, delays, and disappointments, which test and refine our character. Patience involves a humble reliance on God's providence, maintaining confidence in His ultimate resolution while enduring periods of waiting.

3. **The Function of Patience**: As described in James 1:2-4: "My brethren, count it all joy when ye fall into divers temptations; Knowing this, that the trying of your faith worketh patience. But let patience have her perfect work, that ye may be perfect and entire, wanting nothing." This passage illustrates that patience serves a transformative role in our spiritual development. It refines and perfects our character, smoothing out the rough edges and fostering completeness and maturity.

In summary, patience is not merely about enduring difficulties but is integral to spiritual growth and character development. It enables believers to maintain faith and composure amidst trials, contributing to their overall sanctification and alignment with God's will.

In Colossians 4:2, the apostle Paul underscores the significance of steadfastness in prayer, which demonstrates our commitment to God and is pleasing to Him. The example of Paul and Silas, who remained serene and sang praises even while imprisoned, exemplifies this virtue of patience.

1. **Patience as a Divine Process**: Patience is integral to the way God works within us, as illustrated by Romans 8:28: "And we know that all things work together for good to them that love God, to them who are the called according to his purpose." This passage affirms that God uses all circumstances, including trials, to fulfill His purpose for those who love Him. Patience is required both during periods of trouble (Romans 5:3-4) and during ongoing testing (James 1:12; 5:7), emphasizing its role in spiritual growth and resilience.

2. Biblical Examples of Patience and Impatience:

    - Job: As described in James 5:11 and Job 1:20-22, Job exemplifies patience through his endurance of extreme suffering while maintaining his faith in God.

    - Abraham: In Hebrews 6:13-15, Abraham's patience is highlighted as he waited for the fulfillment of God's promise.

- Noah: Noah preached for 120 years (Genesis 6-10) and demonstrated patience by enduring the lengthy period of waiting before the flood.
- Joseph: From age 17 to 30, Joseph exhibited patience as he faced numerous trials before rising to prominence (Genesis 37:34, 35).
- David: Anointed king at age 25, David patiently waited five years before becoming king at age 30.
- Jesus: In Hebrews 12:2, Jesus is described as enduring the cross, illustrating ultimate patience and perseverance.
- Israel: The Israelites' impatience at Mount Sinai (Exodus 32:1) serves as a cautionary example of the consequences of failing to wait on God.

3. Areas Requiring Patience:
    - Tribulations: Patience is necessary in enduring tribulations (1 Peter 2:20-21).

- Delays: Waiting through delays requires patience (Psalm 27:14; 40:1).
- Injustice and Battles: Patience is essential when facing injustice and conflicts (2 Timothy 2:24-26).
- Obedience: Patience is a key component of faithful obedience (Hebrews 10:36).
- Giving Up: Patience is crucial when confronting the temptation to give up (2 Thessalonians 3:5).

4. Cultivating Patience:
    - Prayer Through Trials: Learning to pray consistently through trials and to run the race of faith with endurance is essential (Hebrews 12:1-2).
    - Gratitude: Expressing thankfulness in all circumstances helps to cultivate a patient attitude (1 Thessalonians 5:18).

These practices and examples collectively demonstrate the necessity and benefits of patience in the Christian life, highlighting its role in spiritual development and perseverance.

Step Five: "Add to Temperance" (Patience)

In anticipating the future rather than dwelling on the past or present difficulties, believers are encouraged to focus on the eternal rewards promised by God. Hebrews 11:16 affirms this perspective: "But now they desire a better country, that is, a heavenly: wherefore God is not ashamed to be called their God: for he hath prepared for them a city." This passage highlights the forward-looking faith of the patriarchs, who anticipated a heavenly homeland and, as a result, were honored by God.

Similarly, James 1:12 underscores the divine reward for those who persevere through trials: "Blessed is the man that endureth temptation: for when he is tried, he shall receive the crown of life, which the Lord hath promised to them that love him." This verse illustrates that patience and endurance in the face of temptation are met with the ultimate reward — the crown of life — promised by God to those who maintain their love and commitment to Him.

Together, these passages affirm that a forward-focused faith and steadfast endurance are integral to receiving God's promises and rewards. The encouragement to look ahead and remain steadfast in trials is central to the Christian experience of faith and spiritual fulfillment.

Step Five: "Add to Temperance" (Patience)

Have you ever experienced a sense that God's timing is excessively prolonged? While it may seem that He is taking His time, it is important to recognize that He is orchestrating all things with perfect wisdom and beauty. The rewards for patiently waiting are substantial. Patience has several transformative effects on our lives. It renews our strength, as stress and impatience can deplete our vitality. Through patience, we are prepared for future challenges, develop trust in God's plans, and demonstrate to the world our strength as Christians.

God's purpose in making us wait is often tied to our personal growth and maturation, which are necessary for fulfilling His divine plan. The myriad of life's challenges—pain, burden, and annoyance—are inevitable. In this context, the practice of self-restraint, as described by Peter, equips us with the power to navigate such difficulties with calm assurance. This power is manifested through enduring patience.

Whereas self-restraint involves managing our responses to immediate situations, patience represents a more profound, enduring aspect of our character. It is the quality that enables sustained self-restraint over extended periods. James underscores that the trials and tribulations we face are instrumental in developing patience, which, in turn, contributes to our spiritual maturity and growth in faith.

Patience is not only a response to current difficulties but also a crucial component of long-term spiritual development.

Chapter Fifteen
Step Six: Add to Patience "Godliness"

Faith serves as the gateway into the family of God and establishes the essential foundation upon which the entirety of our Christian life is constructed. Virtue functions as a safeguard, protecting us from the entanglements and defeats brought about by sin. Knowledge, in turn, provides us with the wisdom and discernment necessary to navigate the complexities of life's challenges and the uncertainties that accompany them. Patience empowers us to endure the process of spiritual maturation, allowing us to trust in God's timing and providence. Throughout this journey, it is His grace that sustains, supports, and preserves us, enabling continued growth and resilience in our faith.

The sixth stage of spiritual maturity is Godliness, which entails conforming one's life and mindset to the example set by Jesus Christ. Godliness represents not merely an inward transformation but an outward orientation of one's life toward demonstrating to the world the true essence of righteous living. It can be practically defined as embodying the attitudes and behaviors of Christ, prioritizing a life directed toward God rather than being driven by worldly desires.

As articulated in Titus 2:11-12: "For the grace of God that bringeth salvation hath appeared to all men, Teaching us that, denying ungodliness and worldly lusts, we should live soberly, righteously, and godly, in this present world."

This passage underscores the role of divine grace in guiding believers toward a life marked by sobriety, righteousness, and godliness in the midst of worldly influences. William Penn further affirms this in his observation that "true godliness does not turn men out of the world but enables them to live better in it and excites their endeavors to mend it." Thus, godliness is not an escape from the world but a transformative power that equips individuals to live virtuously within it, contributing to the betterment of society.

True Godliness versus False Godliness

In 2 Timothy 3:1-5, the Apostle Paul provides a warning concerning the moral and spiritual decline that will characterize the "last days": *"1 This know also, that in the last days perilous times shall come. 2 For men shall be lovers of their own selves, covetous, boasters, proud, blasphemers, disobedient to parents, unthankful, unholy, 3Without natural affection, trucebreakers, false accusers, incontinent, fierce, despisers of those that are good, 4Traitors, heady, high-minded, lovers of pleasures more*

Step Six: Add to Patience "Godliness"

than lovers of God; ⁵Having a form of godliness but denying the power thereof: from such turn away."

This passage contrasts *true godliness* with *false godliness*, the latter being an outward semblance of piety that lacks authentic spiritual power and integrity. False godliness is exemplified by individuals who prioritize personal pleasure over a genuine love for God, engaging in religious practices merely to gain social recognition or to enhance self-glorification. Such individuals maintain only the external appearance of righteousness, void of true devotion or transformative spiritual depth.

Jesus underscores this distinction in Matthew 23:27, when He critiques the religious leaders of His time, stating: *"Woe unto you, scribes and Pharisees, hypocrites! for ye are like unto whited sepulchers', which indeed appear beautiful outward, but are within full of dead men's bones, and of all uncleanness."*

In His teachings, Jesus uses the metaphor of "whitewashed tombs" to highlight the stark difference between outward displays of piety and inward spiritual corruption. This analogy underscores the dissonance between external religiosity and internal moral decay, presenting a vivid illustration of false godliness. Both Jesus and Paul emphasize the critical distinction between a life genuinely rooted in alignment with God's will and a superficial appearance of righteousness. Authentic godliness is not predicated on external actions but on a profound inner transformation, revealing a heart that is fully dedicated to God.

True godliness is characterized by a *God-ward orientation*—an intrinsic desire to seek the approval of God rather than that of humanity. It is grounded in a sincere commitment to follow God's will, with the ultimate aim of pleasing Him in all endeavors. Absent this inward posture, any outward expression of devotion becomes mere hypocrisy, devoid of spiritual integrity or depth.

Scripture frames *the mystery of godliness* as a profound theological concept, often juxtaposed with *the mystery of iniquity*, both of which invite deep spiritual reflection. In 1 Timothy 3:16, we read: "And without controversy, great is the mystery of godliness: God was manifest in the flesh, justified in the Spirit, seen of angels, preached unto the Gentiles, believed on in the world, received up into glory."

This passage highlights the incarnation and divinity of Christ, illustrating the core of godliness as an incomprehensible, divine truth that transcends human understanding. Conversely, 2 Thessalonians 2:7 warns: *"For the mystery of iniquity doth already work: only he who now letteth will let, until he be taken out of the way."*

Here, Paul points to the hidden but active presence of evil in the world, a force that works covertly yet pervasively. The juxtaposition between the mysteries of godliness and iniquity underscores the spiritual tension between righteousness and sin, each possessing hidden depths that require discernment and understanding. Grasping the mystery of godliness is essential for true spiritual development and transformation, as it leads believers beyond surface-level observance into a deeper relationship with God.

Our Great Example of Godliness – Jesus According to 1 Timothy 3:16

In 1 Timothy 3:16, the Apostle Paul underscores the preeminence of godliness, highlighting its extraordinary and awe-inspiring character. The term "great" employed by Paul conveys a sense of profound wonder and reverence associated with godliness. He further encapsulates the transformative impact of Christ's earthly life, presenting it as the ultimate exemplar for believers. Jesus' existence serves as a paragon of a life lived in the flesh yet fully governed by the Spirit.

His earthly sojourn epitomizes godliness in its most unadulterated form, as He adhered unwaveringly to divine law while engaging with humanity, experiencing the same conditions and constraints inherent to human life. Unlike any other, He consistently maintained His integrity, never deviating from righteousness, irrespective of circumstances. His obedience was marked by absolute fidelity—there were no deviations from duty or lapses in vigilance. This unwavering consistency embodies the essence of godliness. In confronting life's challenges, believers are called to emulate Christ's endurance, reflecting upon teachings such as those on patience found in James 1:2-4.

Furthermore, Hebrews 4:15 attests to the fact that Christ, despite being subjected to the full spectrum of human temptations, remained sinless. His capacity to resist temptation and endure suffering without succumbing is presented as the quintessential model of godly living. The experiences of pain, hunger, thirst, loneliness, and sorrow did not serve as excuses for any form of ungodly behavior. Rather, Jesus' life demonstrates that these trials can be confronted with unwavering faithfulness, thereby highlighting the essential spiritual resilience required for authentic godliness.

Jesus was also vindicated by the Holy Spirit, whose presence and empowerment throughout His ministry affirmed His divine nature. The miraculous elements surrounding Christ's life, such as His virgin birth and the fulfillment of messianic prophecies, further corroborate His identity as God incarnate. Most decisively, His resurrection—foretold by Him—serves as irrefutable evidence of His divinity and righteousness.

As stated in Acts 4:12, *"Neither is there salvation in any other: for there is none other name under heaven given among men, whereby we must be saved."* This passage underscores the exclusivity of Christ's role in salvation, positioning Him as the singular mediator through whom humanity can attain reconciliation with God.

Christ's life, death, and resurrection manifest the fullness of godliness, providing believers with the ultimate paradigm for spiritual conduct and the sole avenue to eternal life. His existence is not merely an exemplary model but a transformative call to emulate the Spirit-empowered life He embodied. This transcends admiration and invites active participation in a life aligned with His divine standard.

Watching from Heaven

Throughout His earthly ministry, Jesus had the full attention of heaven, with the celestial realm intently observing His every move. At any moment, the hosts of heaven were ready to intervene on His behalf. During the wilderness temptation and even on the cross, Jesus possessed the authority to summon twelve legions of angels (cf. Matthew 26:53). This divine readiness to assist underscores the magnitude of His mission, as well as the heavenly awareness of its importance.

In Acts 19:15, we see the power of His name, as even evil spirits recognized His authority: "And the evil spirit answered and said, Jesus I know, and Paul I know; but who are ye?"

This acknowledgment further emphasizes Jesus' unparalleled stature, feared and known throughout the spiritual realms. Jesus' ministry was characterized by outreach to the *uttermost*—He preached to those who were least like Him, including Gentiles, women, lepers, and Roman guards. His engagement with society's outcasts and marginalized stands as a profound example of godliness in action. After His resurrection, He commanded His disciples to extend His message to all corners of the earth, compelling all people, regardless of background, to return to God (Acts 1:1-10).

Step Six: Add to Patience "Godliness"

Jesus continues to be believed in and trusted by people across the globe, transcending cultural, social, and economic boundaries. His message resonates universally, drawing individuals from diverse backgrounds—young and old, rich and poor—into unity under His lordship. Now seated in glory, He reigns as the exalted King of Kings and Lord of Lords, exercising the same divine authority that characterized His earthly life and ministry. For believers, the call to godliness involves nothing less than striving to conform one's life to Christ's, living with a God-centered focus rather than a world-centered one.

This pursuit of godliness represents the ultimate aim of the Christian life: to model oneself after Christ, who now reigns in heaven as the supreme embodiment of divine righteousness and love. While the challenge of "measuring up" to Christ may seem daunting, it serves as the essential benchmark for spiritual growth and transformation. To live in godliness is to align one's entire existence with the life of Christ, directing every thought, action, and intention toward God, thereby reflecting the fullness of His character.

Facts about Godliness

Godliness is a profound and formidable pursuit—reserved not for the faint-hearted but for those with the courage and resolve to pursue it. It holds great value, encompassing all aspects of life. In 1 Timothy 4:7-8 and 6:6, Paul offers a compelling exhortation:

1 Timothy 4: 6:6, 7-8, *,"⁶But godliness with contentment is great gain.", "⁷But refuse profane and old wives' fables, and exercise thyself rather unto godliness. ⁸For bodily exercise profiteth little: but godliness is profitable unto all things, having promise of the life that now is, and of that which is to come...*

Paul stresses that the pursuit of godliness is not only beneficial for the present life but also for the life to come. It is a path of spiritual gain, far surpassing worldly endeavors. Jesus provides further clarity: **Matthew 6:33,** *"But seek ye first the kingdom of God, and His righteousness; and all these things shall be added unto you."*

This directive underscores that there are no shortcuts in the pursuit of godliness. The priority must always be to seek God's kingdom and His righteousness, trusting that everything else will follow. Likewise, in **Mark 10:28-30**, Jesus promises an abundant return for those who dedicate their lives to His cause:

Mark 10:28-30, "*²⁸Then Peter began to say unto Him, Lo, we have left all and have followed Thee. ²⁹And Jesus answered and said, Verily I say unto you, There is no man that hath left house, or brethren, or sisters, or father, or mother, or wife, or children, or lands, for my sake, and the gospel's, ³⁰But he shall receive an hundredfold now in this time, houses, and brethren, and sisters, and mothers, and children, and lands, with persecutions; and in the world to come eternal life.*"

Here, Christ assures that while the path of godliness may involve sacrifices, it promises incomparable rewards — both in this life and in eternity. The pursuit of godliness, though demanding, yields far-reaching benefits, encompassing not only spiritual and eternal gain but also profound rewards in the present world.

The pursuit of godliness is not only profitable in this present life but also for the life to come. As Paul states in **Romans 6:22,** "*²²But now being made free from sin, and become servants to God, ye have your fruit unto holiness, and the end everlasting life.*"

Godliness is a way of life that reflects the nature of eternity itself. As **2 Peter 3:10, 14** reminds us, everything in this present world — the universe, the earth, and all its works — will one day be utterly destroyed. In light of this, the question arises: What kind of people ought we to be?

The answer is clear—godliness is the only true wealth worth striving for, as it endures beyond the temporal realm.

Moreover, godliness is not merely an abstract concept but a source of real power in life. Paul warns against those who maintain "a form of godliness" while denying its transformative power (cf. **2 Timothy 3:5**). True godliness contains divine power—when our conduct pleases God, He empowers us to live according to His will.

This divine empowerment is clearly articulated in **Philippians 2:12-13**, where Paul explains that God works in us as we strive to do His will. He strengthens us in our inner being by His Spirit (cf. **Ephesians 3:16**), granting us a power beyond comprehension (cf. **Ephesians 3:20**) and enabling us to stand firm in His might (cf. **Ephesians 6:10-13**). If we desire God's power to manifest in our daily lives, godliness is not optional—it is essential. Yet, godliness does not come automatically, nor is it an innate trait. It must be learned and cultivated through proper instruction and intentional practice. True godliness is the result of continuous spiritual formation, grounded in right teaching and deliberate action. Only through this process can believers experience the fullness of godliness, both now and in the life to come.

Step Six: Add to Patience "Godliness"

In 1Timothy 6:3-11, *"³If any man teach otherwise, and consent not to wholesome words, even the words of our Lord Jesus Christ, and to the doctrine which is according to godliness; ⁴He is proud, knowing nothing, but doting about questions and strifes of words, whereof cometh envy, strife, railings, evil surmisings, ⁵Perverse disputings of men of corrupt minds, and destitute of the truth, supposing that gain is godliness: from such withdraw thyself. ⁶But godliness with contentment is great gain. ⁷For we brought nothing into this world, and it is certain we can carry nothing out. ⁸And having food and raiment let us be therewith content. ⁹But they that will be rich fall into temptation and a snare, and into many foolish and hurtful lusts, which drown men in destruction and perdition. ¹⁰For the love of money is the root of all evil: which while some coveted after, they have erred from the faith, and pierced themselves through with many sorrows ¹¹But thou, O man of God, flee these things; and follow after righteous - ness, godliness, faith, love, patience, meekness."*

We acquire godliness through the deliberate and patient endurance of trials, as it is in these crucibles of life that godliness is cultivated. Central to this process is the virtue of patience, upon which godliness is constructed.

There are no shortcuts in this spiritual formation; rather, godliness is progressively integrated into our character, one experience at a time, through perseverance and steadfastness.

Each trial offers an opportunity for growth, shaping us into the likeness of Christ and deepening our capacity for godly living.

Godliness Shows

In every observable aspect of our lives, we are called to reflect either godliness or worldliness. This is evident in the way we speak—whether our words are shaped by godly wisdom or by worldly influences. It is seen in our generosity—whether we give liberally or selfishly. It is also manifested in how we present ourselves—whether we dress with modesty or conform to worldly standards. The manner in which we love others—whether selflessly or with selfish motives—further reveals the depth of our godliness.

Additionally, it is reflected in our thoughts and feelings—whether we focus on the well-being of others or remain consumed by self-interest. Ultimately, the way we face death speaks volumes—whether we do so with expectant peace, as if merely falling asleep in Christ, or with fear and uncertainty, feeling lost and without hope. Each of these dimensions of life reveals the extent to which godliness permeates our character.Growing in Godliness, Requires exercise... strenuous effort on our part, as Paul told according to 1 Timothy 4:7-8, *"7But refuse*

Step Six: Add to Patience "Godliness"

*profane and old **wives**' fables, and exercise thyself rather unto godliness. ⁸For bodily exercise profiteth little: but godliness is profitable unto all things, having promise of the life that now is, and of that which is to come."*

Just as physical exercise contributes to the well-being of the body, spiritual discipline is even more critical for the cultivation of godly living. The spiritual exercises necessary for this growth are outlined in **1 Timothy 4:12-16**: *"¹²Let no man despise thy youth; but be thou an example of the believers, in word, in conversation, in charity, in spirit, in faith, in purity. ¹³Till I come, give attendance to reading, to exhortation, to doctrine. ¹⁴Neglect not the gift that is in thee, which was given thee by prophecy, with the laying on of the hands of the presbytery. ¹⁵Meditate upon these things; give thyself wholly to them; that thy profiting may appear to all. ¹⁶Take heed unto thyself, and unto the doctrine; continue in them: for in doing this thou shalt both save thyself, and them that hear thee."*

Paul exhorts Timothy to engage in spiritual exercises that encompass various dimensions of Christian conduct—exemplifying godliness in speech, behavior, love, spirit, faith, and purity. Attending to the regular reading of Scripture, exhortation, and sound doctrine forms the foundation of spiritual growth. Furthermore, Paul encourages the active use of spiritual gifts, emphasizing the importance of perseverance and meditation on these disciplines. Such spiritual exercise, when pursued with diligence and devotion, not only leads to personal salvation but also benefits those who observe and are influenced by one's godly example.

Strive to be a consistently exemplary model of Christian living for others. Dedicate yourself to the disciplined study of Scripture, with particular focus on reading the Word of God, exhortation through preaching, and learning sound doctrine, which leads to a correct understanding of truth. Maximize your talents and opportunities to serve as a blessing to others, and actively work out your faith. Prioritize living toward God in all things, so that your spiritual growth becomes evident to all. As Peter instructs, this pursuit requires "giving all diligence" (2 Peter 1:5):

2 Peter 1:5 *"And beside this, giving all diligence, add to your faith virtue; and to virtue knowledge."*

This commitment also demands abstinence from engaging in disputes and arguments over mere words. Paul warns against such distractions in **1 Timothy 6:3-4**, *"³If any man teach otherwise, and consent not to wholesome words, even the words of our Lord Jesus Christ, and to the doctrine which is according to godliness; ⁴He is proud, knowing nothing,* *but doting about questions and strifes of words, whereof cometh envy, strife, railings, evil surmisings."*

Likewise, Paul admonishes believers to avoid those who engage in endless word wrangling, as seen in **1 Timothy 6:5**:*"Perverse disputings of men of corrupt minds, and destitute of the truth, supposing that gain is godliness: from such withdraw thyself."*

Moreover, Christians must remain vigilant against materialism and the love of money, understanding that such pursuits are contrary to godliness. As Paul emphasizes in **1 Timothy 6:6-10**, true contentment is found in godliness:*"⁶But godliness with contentment is great gain. ⁷For we brought nothing into this world, and it is certain we can carry nothing out. ⁸And having food and raiment let us be therewith content. ⁹But they that will be rich fall into temptation and a snare, and into many foolish and hurtful lusts, which drown men in destruction and perdition. ¹⁰For the love of money is the root of all evil: which while some coveted after, they have erred from the faith and pierced themselves through with many sorrows."*

In fleeing materialism and the love of wealth, the Christian is called to "earnestly pursue godliness," recognizing that true spiritual gain is not found in the accumulation of earthly riches but in a life characterized by contentment, virtue, and alignment with God's will.

This pursuit is explicitly commanded in 1 Timothy 6:11: *"But thou, O man of God, flee these things; and follow after righteousness, godliness, faith, love, patience, meekness."*

This command implies an active and vigorous pursuit—akin to the relentless chase of a police car after a suspect, or the passionate pursuit of a bride by a groom. It conveys the urgency and intensity with which believers must pursue godly living.

It is God's desire that we model our lives after the example of Jesus Christ—thinking and living as He did. This means living with a focus on God, not on the fleeting concerns of the world. The adversary, the devil, will consistently attempt to divert our focus toward worldly matters, failures, and frustrations, distracting us from the Lord. Godliness, however, faces a significant adversary: self-righteousness.

Any focus other than that of Christ is misaligned—a false target and an erroneous goal. As the apostle John warns, we are not to love the world or the things of the world (cf. 1 John 2:15). Our ultimate example of godliness is found in Jesus Christ. His life demonstrates that godliness is not only great but also a source of real power.

Spiritual maturity does not occur instantaneously or automatically; rather, it is cultivated progressively Spiritual maturity does not occur instant- aneously or automatically; rather, it is cultivated progressively through a series of experiences.

This growth is characterized by a gradual accumulation of insights and understandings gained over time, reflecting the incremental development of spiritual depth and maturity. Each experience contributes to this ongoing process, leading to a more profound and comprehensive spiritual maturity.

Chapter Sixteen

Step Seven: and to Godliness "Brotherly kindness" Loving Believers like Family"

The seventh step in the progression toward spiritual maturity is marked by the cultivation of **Brotherly Kindness**, a critical virtue within Christian ethics and moral theology. According to Webster's Dictionary, "kindness" is defined as an "act of goodwill" or "any act of benevolence which promotes the happiness or welfare of others." This definition emphasizes kindness as an intentional and altruistic behavior aimed at fostering the well-being of others, reflecting a foundational aspect of moral character.

Furthermore, Webster defines the adjective "kind" as the disposition to "do good for others" and to promote their happiness by granting their requests. This concept also includes having "tenderness or goodness of nature" and being inherently benevolent. Such qualities reflect an inward orientation toward compassion and empathy, which are essential for harmonious social and spiritual relations.

In the biblical text of **2 Peter 1:7**, the term for "brotherly kindness" is rendered from the Greek word "Philadelphia," signifying "brotherly love."

This term encapsulates the theological imperative of demonstrating love and care for others within the Christian community, transcending mere emotional affection and embodying a deliberate commitment to serve and support fellow believers.

An examination of the ministry of Jesus Christ provides a clear illustration of this virtue in action. Jesus consistently exemplified kindness in His interactions with others, displaying a mindful concern for the needs and welfare of those around Him. He actively engaged in acts of compassion, healing, and provision, demonstrating a benevolent nature that sought to uplift and restore. In this way, Brotherly Kindness in the life of Christ is revealed not merely as a passive feeling but as an active, outward expression of love and goodness, fulfilling the moral and spiritual ideal of Philadelphia.

Christians Are to Be Kind to All Men,

Jesus serves as the quintessential example for all believers, embodying the moral and spiritual ideals to which Christians are called to aspire. The term "Christian" itself, derived from the Greek (Christianos), literally means "follower of Christ" or "like Christ." This designation implies not merely an identification with Jesus but a moral and ethical imperative to emulate His life and actions.

Step Seven and to Godliness "Brotherly kindness" Loving Believers like Family"

To truly claim the title of Christian, one must strive to live as He lived, walk as He walked, and act as He acted, embodying the virtues He demonstrated throughout His ministry.

The Apostle Paul reinforces this notion in his epistolary exhortation, urging believers to "be kind to one another, tender-hearted, forgiving one another" (Ephesians 4:32). This directive underscores the essential qualities of kindness, compassion, and forgiveness as central to the Christian moral framework. The call to imitate Christ is not simply an abstract theological concept but a practical guide for interpersonal conduct, rooted in love, mercy, and empathy. As followers of Christ, Christians are thus obligated to align their behavior with the example set by Jesus, manifesting these virtues in their daily interactions with others.

According to Ephesians 4:32, a person who embodies kindness actively seeks opportunities to be a blessing to others, constantly on the lookout for ways to engage in benevolent acts. The passage reads: *"And be ye kind one to another, tenderhearted, forgiving one another, even as God for Christ's sake hath forgiven you."*

This biblical exhortation emphasizes the moral and spiritual responsibility of Christians to cultivate a heart of compassion and forgiveness, mirroring the grace that God has extended to humanity through Christ. Kindness, as described here, is not a passive virtue but an active pursuit—Christians are called to intentionally seek out moments to dispense goodness and alleviate the burdens of others.

The question posed about the potential impact of widespread kindness within the Christian community invites reflection on the profound testimony such behavior would bear. If the majority of Christians genuinely walked in kindness, the church's witness in the world would be immeasurably strengthened. The transformative power of Christians embodying God's love, seeking daily to meet the needs of others, would not only reflect the heart of Christ but would also address a pressing societal need for compassion and empathy.

In a world where acts of kindness are increasingly scarce, the church is called to be a beacon of love and a consistent example of benevolence. God orchestrates divine appointments, positioning His followers to encounter the hurting, the lost, and the needy. He expects Christians to put into practice the teachings they have received, to embody the virtues of love and kindness, and to respond to these opportunities with readiness and grace. At such a crucial time in history, the church must rise to the occasion, embracing its mission to be a force of good, meeting the physical and spiritual needs of those around them.

Proverbs 19:22 states, "*The desire of a man is his kindness,*" emphasizing the intrinsic human inclination towards benevolence. This principle is deeply rooted in Christian theology, particularly as articulated in John 13:34-35, where Jesus provides a distinctively Christian ethic: "*A new commandment I give unto you, that ye love one another; as I have loved you, that ye also love one another. By this shall all men know that ye are my disciples, if ye have love one to another.*"

The concept of kindness, therefore, is not merely a general moral virtue but is framed within a uniquely Christian context, wherein believers are commanded to demonstrate love and kindness toward one another as members of a spiritual family. Before extending this love to all humanity, Scripture instructs Christians to prioritize their love and kindness toward their fellow believers, treating them as "family." In 1 Peter 2:17, the Apostle Peter exhorts, "*Honour all men. Love the brotherhood. Fear God. Honour the king,*" while in 1 Peter 3:8, he urges, "*Be ye all of one mind, having compassion one of another, love as brethren, be pitiful, be courteous.*"

These passages underscore the importance of cultivating unity, compassion, and mutual respect within the Christian community.

The Apostle Paul reinforces this idea in Romans 12:10, where he writes, "*Be kindly affectioned one to another with brotherly love; in honour preferring one another.*" Similarly, in Galatians 6:10, Paul emphasizes the need for Christians to prioritize kindness toward their fellow believers: "*As we have therefore opportunity, let us do good unto all men, especially unto them who are of the household of faith.*"

This directive highlights the importance of preferential care for those within the Christian community, suggesting that believers are to place the needs of the "brethren" above personal desires or the demands of the broader public.

In his letter to the Colossians, Paul further instructs Christians to set their minds not on earthly concerns but on higher virtues, urging them to "*put on tender mercies, kindness, humility, meekness, longsuffering; bearing with one another, and forgiving one another, if anyone has a complaint against another; even as Christ forgave you, so you also must do*" (Colossians 3:12-13). Here, Paul calls for a life characterized by mercy and kindness, grounded in the example of Christ's own forgiveness.

This emphasis on mutual care and kindness within the Christian community forms the bedrock of Christian ethical behavior, reinforcing the idea that love for the brethren is the foundation upon which broader acts of kindness to humanity are built.

In **Colossians 3:12-14**, the Apostle Paul offers additional guidance for Christian conduct: *"Put on therefore, as the elect of God, holy and beloved, bowels of mercies, kindness, humbleness of mind, meekness, longsuffering; forbearing one another, and forgiving one another, if any man have a quarrel against any: even as Christ forgave you, so also do ye. And above all these things put on charity, which is the bond of perfectness."*

Here, Paul instructs Christians to "put on" a series of virtues, including kindness, humility, and patience, as a reflection of their identity as God's chosen people. These virtues are not optional but are integral to living a life that reflects Christ's forgiveness and love. Notably, Paul underscores that **love (charity)** is the supreme virtue, binding all others together in a harmonious and complete moral character.

The expectation of Christian kindness extends beyond mere goodwill towards fellow believers. According to **Luke 6:27-36**, Christians are called to love their enemies, bless those who curse them, and show kindness even to those who are ungrateful or evil.

This radical expression of kindness exemplifies the depth of love to which believers are called, aligning their conduct with the divine mercy and grace demonstrated by Christ.

Brotherly kindness is not merely suggested but commanded as part of the Christian ethical framework. In addition to Peter's directive to add brotherly kindness to one's faith (2 Peter 1:7), Paul reinforces this in **Romans 12:10**, urging believers to *"Be kindly affectioned one to another with brotherly love; in honour preferring one another."* This verse emphasizes the need for Christians to prioritize mutual respect and affection within the community of faith, placing the needs of others before their own.

The question of "Who is my brother?" is clarified in Paul's writings. In **Romans 8:16-17**, Paul states that *"The Spirit Himself bears witness with our spirit that we are children of God, and if children, then heirs — heirs of God and joint heirs with Christ, if indeed we suffer with Him, that we may also be glorified together."* Here, Paul affirms that fellow Christians, as children of God, are spiritual siblings and joint heirs with Christ. This familial bond among believers forms the foundation for the call to brotherly kindness.

Paul frequently addressed the Christian community as "brethren" in his epistles, reinforcing the concept of spiritual kinship. This can be seen in his letters to the Philippians (Philippians 3:1), the Colossians (Colossians 4:15), and the Ephesians (Ephesians 6:10), where he consistently urges mutual love and kindness within the household of faith. Thus, the ethical imperative to practice kindness begins within the Christian community, extending outward as a testimony of the transformative power of Christ's love.

As Christians, we share the same Heavenly Father, which establishes a profound spiritual unity among us. This unity is further reinforced by our status as heirs to the same inheritance, as outlined in Scripture. The ability to love is divinely imparted to all believers, as **Romans 5:5** declares, *"the love of God is shed abroad in our hearts by the Holy Ghost."* Therefore, the call to love is not merely aspirational but achievable through the indwelling of God's Spirit. As such, Christians are exhorted to actively practice love and kindness toward one another as a manifestation of their faith.

An exemplary model of brotherly kindness is found in the life of **Joseph**. Despite being hated by his brothers, who sold him into slavery out of jealousy, Joseph ultimately demonstrated extraordinary compassion and forgiveness. When his brothers came to Egypt seeking food during a famine, Joseph had the opportunity to repay their cruelty but instead chose mercy. After the death of their father, Joseph's brothers feared that he might now seek retribution for their past wrongdoing.

This fear is evident in **Genesis 50:15**, where it is written, *"And when Joseph's brethren saw that their father was dead, they said, 'Joseph will peradventure hate us, and will certainly requite us all the evil which we did unto him.'"* However, Joseph's response reveals his deep understanding of divine providence and his commitment to forgiveness. Rather than repaying evil with evil, Joseph recognized God's larger plan and extended grace to his brothers.

Joseph's story illustrates the Christian principle that **unforgiveness** is a tool of Satan, employed to create division and foster a lack of love. When Christians harbor unforgiveness, they fail to reflect the love of Christ and allow Satan to manipulate their emotions and responses. Forgiveness, by contrast, is a hallmark of spiritual maturity and an essential component of brotherly kindness. It breaks the cycle of resentment and retaliation, allowing the love of God to flourish within the Christian community.

In this light, Christians are called to reject unforgiveness and, like Joseph, to respond to offense with love and mercy. Brotherly kindness is not merely an act of goodwill but a reflection of the transformative power of God's love within us, enabling believers to transcend human inclinations toward vengeance and embrace the higher calling of forgiveness and reconciliation.

In **Genesis 50:21**, Joseph demonstrates profound brotherly love, saying to his brothers, *"Now therefore fear ye not: I will nourish you, and your little ones."* The text continues, *"And he comforted them, and spake kindly unto them."* Here, Joseph, despite having been grievously wronged by his brothers, embodies the essence of brotherly kindness. He not only forgives but goes further, providing for their needs and speaking words of comfort, illustrating the depth of compassion that is expected within the Christian ethic of love and forgiveness.

The parable of the **Good Samaritan** in **Luke 10** offers another instructive example of kindness, taught by Jesus Himself. In the parable, several individuals, including a priest and a Levite—both men expected to embody righteousness—pass by a wounded man without offering assistance. It is the Samaritan, a figure traditionally viewed with contempt by the Jewish audience, who stops and shows compassion.

Luke 10:33 records, *"But a certain Samaritan, as he journeyed, came where he was: and when he saw him, he had compassion on him."*

The Samaritan's compassion extends beyond mere sympathy. He tends to the wounded man's injuries, using oil and wine to heal his wounds, places him on his own animal, and takes him to an inn where he pays for his care. This act of kindness is both sacrificial and comprehensive, illustrating the standard of love Christians are called to exhibit, particularly toward those in need. This parable underscores that kindness is not just an emotion but a tangible, selfless act of service, and while this kindness is to be extended universally, it is to be especially directed toward fellow believers.

When considering **how brethren ought to treat one another**, Scripture consistently calls for kindness, affection, and care within the community of faith.

In **Exodus 2:11-13**, we find an example of Israelites failing to show kindness to one another. Moses witnesses two Hebrew men quarreling, reflecting the absence of brotherly affection and the division that can arise when kindness is lacking. This contrasts with the Christian standard set forth in the New Testament.

In **Ephesians 4:32**, Paul commands, *"And be ye kind one to another, tenderhearted, forgiving one another, even as God for Christ's sake hath forgiven you."*

This verse encapsulates the essence of Christian interpersonal relationships—kindness and forgiveness are to be the foundational behaviors that characterize believers' interactions with one another. Brotherly kindness, as modeled by Joseph, the Good Samaritan, and commanded by Paul, is not merely an option but a moral obligation for all who seek to live according to the teachings of Christ. Through kindness, the love of God is made manifest, fostering unity, compassion, and spiritual growth within the body of Christ.

Believers must recognize that we are not in competition with one another. The **parable of the talents** in **Matthew 25** illustrates that the individuals entrusted with various amounts of resources were not competing to see who could accumulate the most wealth. Rather, each was tasked with maximizing the potential of what they had been given. This underscores that our spiritual endeavors are not to be viewed through a lens of rivalry but as opportunities for faithful stewardship, each according to their gifts and abilities.

As Christians, we are called to work toward a common goal, not for individual gain, but as **heirs of the same inheritance**, as seen in **Acts 2:44-45** and **Acts 4:32**, where the early believers shared all things in common and supported one another out of love and unity. The spirit of mutual encouragement is further emphasized in **Hebrews 10:24-25**, where the writer urges believers to "consider one another to provoke unto love and to good works," highlighting that the Christian life is one of cooperation, not competition.

Therefore, our task is not to surpass one another but to **encourage one another** in the faith, fostering a community marked by kindness and mutual support. **Brotherly kindness** is a vital aspect of this, and it must be actively cultivated as part of our spiritual growth. As **John** wrote in **1 John 5:2**, *"By this we know that we love the children of God (our brethren), when we love God and keep His commandments."* This love for God naturally extends into love for our brethren, creating an environment where brotherly kindness flourishes.

Moreover, while we are called to "do good to all men," we are instructed in **Galatians 6:10** to prioritize kindness and care for those who belong to the "household of faith."

This principle underlines the importance of fostering a loving and supportive community among believers. Finally, the simple yet profound exhortation in **Hebrews 13:1** — "Let brotherly love continue" — serves as a reminder that kindness, love, and unity are not just ideals to be aspired to but are commandments to be lived out continually within the body of Christ.

In essence, Christian conduct should not be characterized by competition but by cooperation, mutual encouragement, and a shared pursuit of spiritual maturity. In doing so, we reflect the love of God and embody the spirit of **brotherly kindness** that Scripture so clearly commands.

Why is it essential for Christians to walk in and exhibit brotherly kindness? The answer lies in the foundational truths of our faith: We share the same Heavenly Father, we serve the same Lord — Jesus Christ — and we belong to the same family, the family of God. As pilgrims traveling through this temporal world, we are bound by the same destiny and are heirs of the same eternal inheritance.

In our witness to the world, superficial symbols of faith — such as Christian screensavers, bumper stickers, or music — are not what truly matter. What people genuinely seek is the tangible evidence of Christ alive within us.

They are not as interested in hearing us *speak* about Christ as they are in seeing us *live* like Christ in our daily lives. The greatest testimony a believer can offer is not found in words but in actions that reflect the love of God.

Walking in love and demonstrating **kindness** to others is the most powerful witness of Christ's presence in the world. When we embody the love of God in our relationships and interactions, we provide others with a living image of Christ. Through such actions, people are able to glimpse the transformative power of Christ, made visible through the lives of His followers. Therefore, brotherly kindness is not only an internal Christian virtue but also a critical means through which the world encounters the reality of Jesus Christ.

Chapter Seventeen

Step Seven: and to "Brotherly kindness" (Charity-Agape Love)

There is no love greater than God's love! Love is the law that governs the operation of blessings; therefore, love is the commandment of God. In order to experience God's love for us we must get to know God and build a relationship with God. Stay faithful and trust God. We are always wanting and needing something from God without really knowing who God is.

Once you learn to walk in love and continue walking in love, you will also have faith, righteousness, healing, prosperity, and gifts of the Holy Spirit. When we walk outside of love, we began to walk into darkness. Darkness is cursed, as believers, we belong in the light. We are born of light because we are born of God, and just as God is light, God is love. Pursue God, build a relationship, and walk in love. Your life will be blessed beyond your imagination.

I believe the message of God's Love is one of the most important massage in the Bible. Many times when a person is a born-again they try to live the Christian life based upon the love that the world has to offer.

Step Seven: and to "Brotherly kindness"
(Charity-Agape Love)

In the Kingdom of God there is a new type of love "Agape" that has been placed in our hearts when we are born again, according to Romans 5:5. *"And hope maketh not ashamed; because the love of God is shed abroad in our hearts by the Holy Ghost which is given unto us."*

I heard this statement and I believe it is true "What you do not understand you will misuse and abuse!"

To walk in THE BLESSING, everything must hang the rod on love. The faith that connects us to it "worketh by love." The fear that disconnects us from it is cast out by love. Walking in love keeps us flowing in THE BLESSING and out of the darkness of the curse. For "He that loveth, abideth in the light, and there is no occasion of stumbling."

I heard a Pastor tell the story of a man who had a vision from the Lord. In the vision, the man was attempting to hang a big and beautiful curtains but the curtain rod kept falling down. After a few tries he realized that each of the curtains had meaningful words on them. The words were faith, righteousness, healing, prosperity and gifts of the Holy Spirit.

Step Seven: and to "Brotherly kindness" (Charity-Agape Love)

The man in the vision became frustrated because no matter how hard he tried the curtains would not stay in place. While he worked on one curtain, another curtain would fall. The man finally cried out to the Lord in desperation, and the Lord responded, "Hang the rod!" He looked over and saw a huge golden rod. The rod was big enough to hold all the curtains in place. The rod also had words on it that read, "The Love of God."

I may not have told the story exactly the way that Pastor Winston told it, but the essence is there. In the Kingdom of God, everything hangs on the rod of love or the love of God. Once you get the rod of love in place along with the curtains of faith, righteousness, healing, prosperity and the gifts of the spirit, everything will hang in place as it should.

Trying to receive the blessings of God without the love of God can be a frustrating experience. Too many people are trying to get things from God without really knowing God at all. Don't pursue things, pursue God. If you pursue God and walk in love of God, blessings will come to you. Nothing else really works without the love of God operating in your life. Jesus simplified the message of the Bible for us in two commandments: love God and love man.

Step Seven: and to "Brotherly kindness" (Charity-Agape Love)

If you can do these two things, then you are giving God His proper place in your life, and you are, in effect, hanging the rod of love.

Once you have love in place, everything else will stay in place. Love is not just a good idea or a suggestion. Love is THE commandment of God because love is THE law that governs the operation of THE BLESSING.

To fully understand what that means, you must remember that the word law can be defined in two ways. First, there are irrefutable laws such as the laws of nature. Those laws are truth. They cannot be changed, and they always work. The law of physics and mathematics fall into that category. It doesn't matter what form government is in power or what kind of rules men might come up with, irrefutable laws can't be altered.

Congress could pass a law declaring two plus two is five but that wouldn't make it so. The Supreme Court could declare that the law of gravity has been canceled, but it wouldn't matter. Things will still hit the floor when you drop them because gravity always works, and no government on earth can change that.

Step Seven: and to "Brotherly kindness" (Charity-Agape Love)

Although most people think irrefutable laws apply only to the natural realm. The realm of the spirit is also governed by such laws. The spiritual world is not a place where just anything goes. Its laws are even more exact than natural, physical laws. That's not surprising because God, who is a Spirit, created all earthly matter. He patterned the physical world after the spiritual world.

"Faith cometh by hearing, and hearing by The WORD of God" Romans 3:27 calls that "the law of faith." It goes into operation when two elements come together a hearer and The WORD of God always produces the same thing: faith.

It doesn't matter who you are, who your parents are, whether you are a man or woman, or what color your skin is, the law of faith works the same way for everyone, all the time. A law that works right alongside the law of faith is found in *Galatians 5:6.*

Galatians 5:6, *"For in Jesus Christ neither circumcision availeth anything, nor uncircumcision; but faith which worketh by love."*

That is a practical, unalterable truth. There's nothing religious or abstract about it. Faith works by love like a car works by gasoline. No gas, no go. No love, no faith. No faith, no receiving.

Step Seven: and to "Brotherly kindness" (Charity-Agape Love)

Like the law of gravity, faith worketh by love is an irrefutable, spiritual law.

The second type of law that exists both in the natural and the spiritual realms is governmental laws. Governmental laws are commands put into effect and enforced by the legal authorities of the land. It is possible to break them, but you will experience consequences. If you run a red light, you'll get a ticket. Steal a car and you'll go to jail. God's governmental laws are called commandments. People can and do break them; and when they do, it's called sin. As I've said before, there have been great and absurd debates about what is and is not sin. But the real definition is simple. Sin is violating the established laws of God.

The devil tries to sell the idea that God established those laws because He is mad at us and doesn't want us to have any fun. But that's a lie. God gave them to us to keep us from killing ourselves. He put them in place to protect us because He knows, even if we don't, that "the wages of sin is death." People can argue about it all they want to.

They can mock the dangers of sin and say there's nothing wrong with it. But that won't change the consequences. Sin always does just what God said it will do.

Step Seven: and to "Brotherly kindness"
(Charity-Agape Love)

It sets in motion "the law of sin and death." Sin always leads to death because death is what it produces in the spirit. Adultery, for example, kills. It works death in a family. There's something that happens in the human spirit, soul and body when a person honors satan by giving him reign in that area. People convince themselves they can contain the damage caused by it. But in reality, opening the door to that one sin gives the devil access to their entire life. He'll take advantage of that access, too. That's just the way he is. Every fish in the sea and the sea itself all were made by Love's WORD.

Love created you. Love breathed life into you. Therefore, everything that is contrary to Love goes against your very substance. Every word of disharmony violates the way you were made. Unloving words, thoughts and actions do violence to the very nerves and cells in your physical body.

No wonder Jesus said that love is the greatest commandment! No wonder He made it a command to love The LORD thy God with all your heart, all your soul, your entire mind and all your strength, and also to love your neighbor as yourself!

Step Seven: and to "Brotherly kindness"
(Charity-Agape Love)

When we strive and fuss with others, we become our own worst enemy. We actually begin to self-destruct. When we walk in love, however, we not only BLESS others, but we also edify ourselves.

Ephesians 6:8; says, *"Whatsoever good thing any man doeth, the same shall he receive of The LORD."*

In other words, every act of love, every word of kindness, every loving gesture, enlivens us. The cells in our bodies respond to it. Our minds respond to it. Our spirits expand on the inside of us, strengthening and preparing us to walk in the anointing we were born to carry.

When we take a step outside of love, we step into darkness. That's where the curse is, and it's not where we, as believers, belong. We belong in the light. We are born of light because we are born of God; and just as God is Love, God is Light.'" For ye were sometimes darkness, but now are ye light in The LORD: walk as children of light (*Ephesians 5:8*). The first thing God said at Creation was, "Light be!"

Ephesians 5:8, *"For ye were sometimes darkness, but now are ye light in the Lord: walk as children of light:"*

That's why your physical body is electrically operated, and its battery runs on light. Light is the source of our physical power and light is the source of every act of Love. Now you have been exposed to steps of learning about the highest type of Love, Agape, the love of God that has been shed aboard and poured into your heart by the Holy Spirit; (Romans 5:5).

Romans 5:5, *"And hope maketh not ashamed; because the love of God is shed abroad in our hearts by the Holy Ghost which is given unto us."*

It is very important that you grow and walk in the love of God, because if you fail in this area the other laws will not work because they are all tied to the Royal law of the kingdom which is love. As I mentioned earlier, everything hangs on the Rod of love.

In the English language, we use the one word "love" to express different levels of affection. For example, you might hear someone say, "I love my brother," "I love my mother," I love my wife," "I love candy," I love cars," "I love this," "I love that," and so forth. In each instance, they use the same word: love. You have to look at the context of what the person is saying to understand the kind of love that they are talking about.

The Greek language has four different words that are used to express or define the different kinds of "love."

Step Seven: and to "Brotherly kindness" (Charity-Agape Love)

The first is "**Storge**," which is an affectionate love that exists between parent and child, loyal citizens and rulers, and so forth.

The second is "**Eros**," which refers to physical love arising out of passion.
The third Greek word for love is "**Phileo**," which is a love that cherishes. An example of this is the love for a brother or a friend.

All of these loves – Storge, Eros, and Phileo – should be based on the fourth Greek word for love – "**Agape**"

The highest kind of love is God's kind of love, a love that is not based on feeling or performances, but a decision. Agape is a selfless, sacrificial love that goes far beyond anything that most people can even come close to understanding.

When some people are asked to do something for someone else, the first thing they want to know is what I will get in return for doing it. But God's kind of love gives. True love – Agape love does not concern itself with, "What am I going to get out of it?" No, it concerns itself with, "What will this other person gain by me loving them?"

In Ephesians 5:25 - 40, Paul tells the husband to love their wives as Christ loved the church. Well, how did Christ love the church? He gave Himself for it, and that's the way we are to love we are to give.

Ephesians 5:25-40, "*Husbands, love your wives, even as Christ also loved the church, and gave himself for it; ^{26} That he might sanctify and cleanse it with the washing of water by the word, ^{27} That he might present it to himself a glorious church, not having spot, or wrinkle, or any such thing; but that it should be holy and without blemish. ^{28} So ought men to love their wives as their own bodies. He that loveth his wife loveth himself. ^{29} For no man ever yet hated his own flesh; but nourisheth and cherisheth it, even as the Lord the church: ^{30} For we are members of his body, of his flesh, and of his bones. ^{31} For this cause shall a man leave his father and mother, and shall be joined unto his wife, and they two shall be one flesh. ^{32} This is a great mystery: but I speak concerning Christ and the church. ^{33} Nevertheless let every one of you in particular so love his wife even as himself; and the wife see that she reverence her husband.*

Proverbs 12:4, "*A virtuous woman is a crown to her husband: but she that maketh ashamed is as rottenness in his bones.*"

In John 3:16, we have a great example of Agape love.

Step Seven: and to "Brotherly kindness"
(Charity-Agape Love)

It says, "For God so LOVED the world, that HE GAVE his only begot Son (JESUS), that whosoever believeth in him should not perish, but have everlasting life." God's kind of love will love a person even if that person does not want to be loved. (Emphasis Add)

Agape love, or God's kind of love, even loves a person who doesn't seem to deserve love because of what that person does or says. God's kind of love loves people regardless of their actions. Agape love, it doesn't matter who you are or what you do or what you have done. You can still be loved by the power of God and receive Jesus as your Savior.

As God's children, we must grow and walk in the love of God. As humans, we experience different types of love. We experience love that shows affection between parents and their children, physical love that's filled with passion, a love that cherishes a brother or a friend, and then God's love.

There is no greater love! God loves us unconditionally. He loves us even when we don't deserve to be loved. In order to be in a position to Yoke up with Jesus and the Kingdom of God Government we must walk and continue to walk in the love of God.

Step Seven: and to "Brotherly kindness"
(Charity-Agape Love)

Matthew 22:37-40, *"Jesus said unto him, Thou shalt love the Lord thy God with all thy heart, and with all thy soul, and with all thy mind. [38] This is the first and great commandment. [39] And the second is like unto it, Thou shalt love thy neighbour as thyself. [40] On these two commandments hang all the law and the prophets.* John 15:12, *"This is my commandment, that ye love one another, as I have loved you."*

Remember
What you do not understand you will misuse and abuse!

Decision Page

As previously discussed regarding Jesus' invitation to "Come and learn of Me," the pathway to experiencing and walking in the blessings of God fundamentally requires receiving Jesus Christ as one's personal Lord and Savior. This personal acceptance is essential for accessing and embodying the divine blessings and promises articulated in the teachings of Christ.

Jesus said, *"except you are born again yea shall not see the Kingdom of God" (John 3:3).*

To experience the blessings of God as outlined in this booklet and throughout the Holy Bible, it is essential to be born again. According to Colossians 1:12, this rebirth qualifies you to partake in the wonderful inheritance that God has prepared for you.

Below are several scripture references that you can consult to substantiate these claims. Additionally, a brief prayer is provided to guide you in receiving the Lord Jesus Christ as your personal Lord and Savior. Through this act, you will be born into the Kingdom of God. The transformative power of God's Word has the capacity to profoundly alter your life, renew your heart, and secure your eternal destiny.

Receiving Jesus Christ as Your Personal Lord and Savior

Are you born again?

If you have not yet received Jesus as your personal Lord and Savior, it is essential to consider the following scriptural references and prayer. Reflect on these verses, and if you believe them with your heart, pray the accompanying prayer.

Scriptural References:

- *John 3:16* – "For God so loved the world, that He gave His only begotten Son, that whosoever believeth in Him should not perish, but have everlasting life."
- *Romans 10:9-10, 13* – "That if thou shalt confess with thy mouth the Lord Jesus, and shalt believe in thine heart that God hath raised Him from the dead, thou shalt be saved. For whosoever shall call upon the name of the Lord shall be saved. For with the heart man believeth unto righteousness; and with the mouth confession is made unto salvation."

By aligning your heart with these truths and praying the following prayer, you can embrace the promise of salvation and enter into a transformative relationship with Jesus Christ.

Prayer for Salvation

Heavenly Father,

I desire to become a citizen of Your Kingdom. I approach You in the name of Jesus, Your Son. I acknowledge that I am a sinner and affirm my belief that You sent Your Son to die on the cross for my sins. I confess with my mouth that Jesus Christ is Lord. Thank You for granting me the privilege of becoming a Christian. I am now transferred from the kingdom of darkness into the Kingdom of Almighty God. In Jesus' name, I pray. Amen.

As a sincere born-again Christian and citizen of the Kingdom of Almighty God, my foremost goal is to fulfill Your will. I commit to boldly witnessing to others and sharing how they can also become Christians. I will join a Bible-believing church and participate in water baptism as an act of faith, publicly declaring my discipleship to Christ. I am committed to receiving the fullness of the Holy Spirit and being guided by Him as I continue to grow spiritually and mature in my relationship with Christ through the study of Your Word.

Signed:_____

Date: _____

Bibliography

1. 21st Century King James Version (KJ21) Copyright © 1994 by Deuel Enterprises, Inc. American Standard Version (ASV) Public Domain (Why are modern Bible translations copyrighted?).
2. Amplified Bible (AMP) Copyright © 2015 by The Lockman Foundation, La Habra, CA 90631. All rights reserved.
3. Amplified Bible, Classic Edition (AMPC) Copyright © 1954, 1958, 1962, 1964, 1965, 1987 by The Lockman Foundation.
4. BRG Bible (BRG) Blue Red and Gold Letter Edition™ Copyright © 2012 BRG Bible Ministries. Used by Permission. All rights reserved. BRG Bible is a Registered Trademark in U.S. Patent and Trademark Office #4145648.
5. Christian Standard Bible (CSB) The Christian Standard Bible. Copyright © 2017 by Holman Bible Publishers. Used by permission. Christian Standard Bible®, and CSB® are federally registered trademarks of Holman Bible Publishers, all rights reserved.
6. Common English Bible (CEB) Copyright © 2011 by Common English Bible.
7. Complete Jewish Bible (CJB) Copyright © 1998 by David H. Stern. All rights reserved.
8. Contemporary English Version (CEV) Copyright © 1995 by American Bible Society.
9. Darby Translation (DARBY) Public Domain (Why are modern Bible translations copyrighted?).

Bibliography

10. Douay-Rheims 1899 American Edition (DRA) Public Domain (Why are modern Bible translations copyrighted?).
11. Easy-to-Read Version (ERV) Copyright © 2006 by Bible League International.
12. Evangelical Heritage Version (EHV) The Holy Bible, Evangelical Heritage Version®, EHV®, © 2019 Wartburg Project, Inc. All rights reserved.
13. English Standard Version (ESV) The Holy Bible, English Standard Version. ESV® Text Edition: 2016. Copyright © 2001 by Crossway Bibles, a publishing ministry of Good News Publishers.
14. English Standard Version Anglicised (ESVUK) The Holy Bible, English Standard Version Copyright © 2001 by Crossway Bibles, a division of Good News Publishers.
15. Expanded Bible (EXB) The Expanded Bible, Copyright © 2011 Thomas Nelson Inc. All rights reserved.
16. 1599 Geneva Bible (GNV) Geneva Bible, 1599 Edition. Published by Tolle Lege Press. All rights reserved. No part of this publication may be reproduced or transmitted in any form or by any means, electronic or mechanical, without written permission from the publisher, except in the case of brief quotations in articles, reviews, and broadcasts.
17. GOD'S WORD Translation (GW) Copyright © 1995, 2003, 2013, 2014, 2019, 2020 by God's Word to the Nations Mission Society. All rights reserved.
18. Good News Translation (GNT) Copyright © 1992 by American Bible Society.

Bibliography

19. Holman Christian Standard Bible (HCSB) Copyright © 1999, 2000, 2002, 2003, 2009 by Holman Bible Publishers, Nashville Tennessee. All rights reserved.
20. International Children's Bible (ICB) The Holy Bible, International Children's Bible® Copyright© 1986, 1988, 1999, 2015 by Tommy Nelson™, a division of Thomas Nelson. Used by permission.
21. International Standard Version (ISV) Copyright © 1995-2014 by ISV Foundation. ALL RIGHTS RESERVED INTERNATIONALLY. Used by permission of Davidson Press, LLC.
22. Jubilee Bible 2000 (JUB) Copyright © 2013, 2020 by Ransom Press International.
23. King James Version (KJV) Public Domain. Authorized (King James) Version (AKJV) KJV reproduced by permission of Cambridge University Press, the Crown's patentee in the UK.
24. Lexham English Bible (LEB) 2012 by Logos Bible Software. Lexham is a registered trademark of Logos Bible Software.
25. Living Bible (TLB) The Living Bible copyright © 1971 by Tyndale House Foundation. Used by permission of Tyndale House Publishers Inc., Carol Stream, Illinois 60188. All rights reserved.
26. The Message (MSG) Copyright © 1993, 2002, 2018 by Eugene H. Peterson.
27. Modern English Version (MEV) The Holy Bible, Modern English Version. Copyright © 2014 by Military Bible Association. Published and distributed by Charisma House.

Bibliography

28. Names of God Bible (NOG) The Names of God Bible (without notes) © 2011 by Baker Publishing Group.
29. New American Bible (Revised Edition) (NABRE) Scripture texts, prefaces, introductions, footnotes and cross references used in this work are taken from the New American Bible, revised edition © 2010, 1991, 1986, 1970 Confraternity of Christian Doctrine, Inc., Washington, DC All Rights Reserved. No part of this work may be reproduced or transmitted in any form or by any means, electronic or mechanical, including photocopying, recording, or by any information storage and retrieval system, without permission in writing from the copyright owner.
30. New American Standard Bible (NASB) New American Standard Bible®, Copyright © 1960, 1971, 1977, 1995, 2020 by The Lockman Foundation. All rights reserved.
31. New American Standard Bible 1995 (NASB1995) New American Standard Bible®, Copyright © 1960, 1971, 1977, 1995 by The Lockman Foundation. All rights reserved.
32. New Century Version (NCV) The Holy Bible, New Century Version®. Copyright © 2005 by Thomas Nelson, Inc.
33. New English Translation (NET) NET Bible® copyright ©1996-2017 by Biblical Studies Press, L.L.C. http://netbible.com All rights reserved.

Bibliography

34. New International Reader's Version (NIRV) Copyright © 1995, 1996, 1998, 2014 by Biblica, Inc.®. Used by permission. All rights reserved worldwide.
35. New International Version (NIV) Holy Bible, New International Version®, NIV® Copyright ©1973, 1978, 1984, 2011 by Biblica, Inc.® Used by permission. All rights reserved worldwide.
36. New International Version - UK (NIVUK) Holy Bible, New International Version® Anglicized, NIV® Copyright © 1979, 1984, 2011 by Biblica, Inc.® Used by permission. All rights reserved worldwide.
37. New King James Version (NKJV) Scripture taken from the New King James Version®. Copyright © 1982 by Thomas Nelson. Used by permission. All rights reserved.
38. New Life Version (NLV) Copyright © 1969, 2003 by Barbour Publishing, Inc.
39. New Living Translation (NLT) Holy Bible, New Living Translation, copyright © 1996, 2004, 2015 by Tyndale House Foundation. Used by permission of Tyndale House Publishers, Inc., Carol Stream, Illinois 60188. All rights reserved.
40. New Revised Standard Version (NRSV) New Revised Standard Version Bible, copyright © 1989 the Division of Christian Education of the National Council of the Churches of Christ in the United States of America. Used by permission. All rights reserved.

Bibliography

41. [New Revised Standard Version, Anglicised](#) (NRSVA) New Revised Standard Version Bible: Anglicised Edition, copyright © 1989, 1995 the Division of Christian Education of the National Council of the Churches of Christ in the United States of America. Used by permission. All rights reserved.
42. [New Revised Standard Version, Anglicised Catholic Edition](#) (NRSVACE) New Revised Standard Version Bible: Anglicised Catholic Edition, copyright © 1989, 1993, 1995 the Division of Christian Education of the National Council of the Churches of Christ in the United States of America. Used by permission. All rights reserved.
43. [New Revised Standard Version Catholic Edition](#) (NRSVCE) New Revised Standard Version Bible: Catholic Edition, copyright © 1989, 1993 the Division of Christian Education of the National Council of the Churches of Christ in the United States of America. Used by permission. All rights reserved.
44. [Orthodox Jewish Bible](#) (OJB) Copyright © 2002, 2003, 2008, 2010, 2011 by Artists for Israel International.
45. [The Passion Translation](#) (TPT) The Passion Translation®. Copyright © 2017, 2018, 2020 by Passion & Fire Ministries, Inc. Used by permission. All rights reserved. thePassionTranslation.com.

Bibliography

46. Revised Standard Version (RSV) Revised Standard Version of the Bible, copyright © 1946, 1952, and 1971 the Division of Christian Education of the National Council of the Churches of Christ in the United States of America. Used by permission. All rights reserved.
47. Revised Standard Version Catholic Edition (RSVCE) The Revised Standard Version of the Bible: Catholic Edition, copyright © 1965, 1966 the Division of Christian Education of the National Council of the Churches of Christ in the United States of America. Used by permission. All rights reserved.
48. Tree of Life Version (TLV) Tree of Life (TLV) Translation of the Bible. Copyright © 2015 by The Messianic Jewish Family Bible Society.
49. The Voice (VOICE) The Voice Bible Copyright © 2012 Thomas Nelson, Inc. The Voice™ translation © 2012 Ecclesia Bible Society All rights reserved.
50. **World English Bible** (WEB) by Public Domain. The name "World English Bible" is trademarked.
51. **Wycliffe Bible** (WYC) 2001 by Terence P. Noble. Young's Literal Translation (YLT) by Public Domain

PARTNERSHIP

Pastor James L. Monteria, an anointed teacher of the Word of God, has over three decades of dedicated service in ministry, consistently upholding and imparting the enduring truths of Scripture. His ministry spans diverse platforms, including church services, Bible studies, prison outreach, academic seminars, and evangelistic crusades, alongside the dissemination of theological resources through books, CDs, and DVDs. Pastor Monteria's theological foundation is firmly anchored in a deep conviction of the Holy Spirit's guidance, which informs both his homiletic and didactic approaches, allowing him to convey the profound truths of Scripture with clarity, precision, and spiritual authority.

PARTNERSHIP

Pastor Monteria completed his ministerial training at Rhema Bible Training Center College in Broken Arrow, Oklahoma. He also holds a Bachelor of Science in Business Administration from Saint Paul's College in Lawrenceville, Virginia, a Master's degree in Instructional Education from Central Michigan University in Mount Pleasant, Michigan, and a Doctoral degree from Virginia Union University in Richmond, Virginia.

Would you like to partner with us for the **'A New Way of Living' training as part of the Harvest discipleship program?** This training is designed for a new generation of ministers filled with the Spirit of God and the wisdom of His word. Consider becoming a partner with Pastor James L. Monteria to help in teaching, training, developing, and sending out equipped Kingdom citizens with character and integrity are disciples

PARTNERSHIP

of Jesus Christ. Your role as a partner with our partnership team is invaluable.

As I did in my previous prison for over 22 years, you may only realize the extent of your impact once you reach heaven. Your prayers and financial support can lead to countless people receiving Jesus, being filled with the Holy Spirit, finding healing, and discovering God's will for their lives.

Your prayers and contributions are profoundly impactful, demonstrating the essential role each partner plays in this collective ministry. The full extent of your influence may only be revealed in eternity, where the lives touched—those who have embraced Christ, been filled with the Holy Spirit, experienced healing, or discovered God's will—will bear testimony to the significance of your spiritual and financial support. To further contribute, please mail your donation to CLM Ministries, P.O. Box 932, Chesterfield, Virginia, 23832 or visit **www.JamesMonteria.com**.

About the Author

CLM Ministries, LLC P. O. Box 932, Chesterfield, VA 23832
Email:
Clmpublication.info@gmial.com
(804)475-3155
www.JamesMonteria.com

As the founder of CLM Publishing, LLC, an extension of CLM Ministries, I have personally navigated the complexities of the publishing industry. My journey as an author was fraught with challenges, including prohibitive costs, the potential loss of rights to my intellectual property, offers of royalties in lieu of direct compensation, and requirements for large purchases without adequate marketing strategies. These obstacles led me to self-publish; a process that proved far more accessible than I had anticipated. Today, I am delighted to extend this same opportunity to help others bring their publishing aspirations to fruition.

There is a book in you! Let us help you PUBLISH it! We can make your Dream book come true.

www.ingramcontent.com/pod-product-compliance
Lightning Source LLC
Chambersburg PA
CBHW061257110426
42742CB00012BA/1953